D0821236

Greek Athletics *and*
The Genesis of Sport

Greek Athletics
and
The Genesis
of Sport

David Sansone

UNIVERSITY OF CALIFORNIA PRESS

Berkeley / Los Angeles / London

University of California Press
Berkeley and Los Angeles, California

University of California Press, Ltd.
London, England

© 1988 by
The Regents of the University of California

Library of Congress Cataloging-in-Publication Data

Sansone, David.
  Greek Athletics and the Genesis of Sport

  Bibliography: p.
  Includes index.
  1. Sports. 2. Sports—Greece—History. I. Sansone,
David. Nature of Greek athletics. 2988. II. Title.
Anatomy of sport. III. Nature of Greek athletics.
GV706.8.S26   1988   796   87-14304
ISBN 0-520-06099-7 (alk. paper)

Printed in the United States of America

1 2 3 4 5 6 7 8 9

*L'originalitat consisteix
a tornar a l'origen.*

—Antoni Gaudí

Contents

List of Illustrations

Prelude

A generation ago there occurred, within a nine-month period, three events that planted the seeds from which the twin essays that comprise this modest book were to spring. On 27 May 1945, at a time when the front pages of newspapers were proclaiming the suicides of high-ranking officials of the defeated German forces, the American classical scholar William Abbott Oldfather died in a boating "accident." On 1 August of the same year, the sixtieth birthday of another classical scholar, Peter von der Mühll, was marked by the dedication of a Festschrift (not actually published until 1946) that included a seminal article by Karl Meuli on the origins of Greek sacrificial practice. Early in the following year my own father, who was not particularly old, committed the rash act that was to result in my birth some months later. There is no need to expatiate at length on the importance of this last event for the genesis of this book. Meuli's "Griechische Opferbräuche" will be referred to below so frequently and in such critical connections that it will be obvious even to the casual reader that the brilliant Swiss scholar is the legitimate πατὴρ τοῦ λόγου. The rôle of Oldfather is somewhat more contingent and circumstantial. Among the numerous accomplishments of this extraordinary man was the creation at the University of Illinois of a course in the sports of ancient Greece and Rome. The aim of this course was, in part, to stem the tide of moral and physical degeneration and to inculcate the healthful lessons offered by the model of Greek athletics. For Oldfather, these lessons were of more than merely historical importance—they were part of the inheritance of race. For, as he told his students (during World War II!), "the Greeks were a Nordic people, most closely related to our Germanic ancestors." At any rate, on Oldfather's death, responsibility for the teaching of this course devolved upon a series of colorless epigoni, of whom I am the latest.

When I inherited the course, my protests that I knew nothing of the subject matter were met with reassurances that whatever could be taught could, under certain circumstances, be learned. Armed with Socratic knowledge of the extent of my ignorance, I immediately, in the words of Richard Watson, applied myself with great eagerness to the study of sports in Greece and Rome. A variety of helpful books quickly remedied my deficiency with regard to the details of the subject in which I was required to pass myself off as an expert. But I did not share Oldfather's confident understanding of the nature of sport, nor was I able to find any book or article that could satisfy my desire to learn whence comes the apparent exhilaration that is associated with sport. Oldfather had been satisfied to explain sport as practice for war, the exhilaration of which, at least among the Greeks and other "Nordic" peoples, needed no explanation: "Blond, tall, muscular, we Nordics are a fighting race, perpetually disturbing the peace of the world, and of one another. War has been with us not merely a necessity but an amusement, a form of entertainment, an exciting way of working off that excess of physical and nervous energy with which our branch of the human race has been endowed" (unpublished lecture notes). My temperament as well as my scholarly instinct inclined me to the belief that a more sophisticated and rigorous approach than Oldfather's was needed, if for no other reason than the desirability of accounting for sport among branches of the human race to which neither he nor I belonged.

I must admit, however, that, when it came time for me to give my first lectures, I had no idea of what sport is or why it is so avidly pursued by so many. I compromised my principles and, instead of delivering what I regarded as a necessary introductory lecture on "The Phenomenology of Sport," I proceeded on the assumption (which it never occurred to my students to question) that both they and I knew perfectly well what sport is. In the course of my lectures, however, it gradually dawned on me that there were a number of curious features, particularly of Greek sport, that had never been adequately explained and that might provide clues to the nature and origin of sport in general. Specifically, I began to notice the intimate connection between Greek athletics and sacrificial ritual, and it occurred to me to wonder whether the athlete was not in some sense regarded as a sacrificial victim. At the same time my understanding of the nature of sacrificial ritual was immeasurably clarified by my reading of the works of Walter Burkert, who alerted me to the significance of the researches of Karl Meuli. All of this led me to formulate the novel definition presented and defended below, namely, that sport is the ritual sacrifice of physical energy. In Part One, "The Genesis of Sport," the case will be made that this is the most, indeed the only, satisfactory definition that has so far been advanced. Part Two, "The Nature of Greek Athletics," examines those features of ancient Greek sport that can best be explained in the light of our newly won understanding of sport. The two essays are complementary in that their respective arguments reinforce each other, and it is hoped that both essays will be of interest to (and accessible to) the reader who is expert neither in the theory of sport nor in the classics. To this end, I have translated all quotations from works not written in English (translations by others are so identified) and, in my citations, have avoided using abbreviations and other forms of reference designed by specialists to intimidate the uninitiated.

Part One

The Genesis of Sport

The Ukrainian word for sport is *spórt*. If you wish to read an account of yesterday's soccer match in an Athenian newspaper, you will look for the pages headed *Spór*. The magnificent building in Rome, designed by Pier Luigi Nervi and Marcello Piacentini, in which Cassius Clay won the gold medal for boxing in the light-heavyweight division at the Olympic Games in 1960 is called the Palazzo dello Sport. There is a Gaelic word *spòrs*, a Turkish word *spor,* a Rumanian word *spórt* and a Japanese word *supōtsu*. The speakers of all these languages, along with those of a host of others, have borrowed the English word *sport* because their native vocabularies did not provide them with a term that conveyed precisely what the English word conveys. This is somewhat surprising. For all these peoples—indeed, apparently, all peoples—traditionally engage in activities of a sort that can conveniently be designated by the word *sport*. Did the ancient Greeks, then, not have a general term to describe such activities as wrestling and throwing the discus? Is there no native Gaelic word that can be used to refer to field hockey and similar games? Was it really necessary for the devotees of sumo to import a Western word? The very ubiquity of the word in the languages of the world gives the answer to these questions: the English word *sport* refers to something for which many languages simply do not have a word. In fact, when we look at the history of the word in English, we find that even English managed to exist for a good long time without a word to refer to what the Dutch call *sport*.[1]

The English word *sport* is not attested before the fifteenth century. It comes from the archaic English word *disport*, which comes, in turn, from the Old French *desport*. The French word, which means "diversion, recreation, pastime, amusement," is formed from the Latin prefix *de(s)-*, meaning "down" or "away from," and the Latin verbal root *port-*, meaning "to carry." Thus the basic reference of the English and French words is to that which draws the attention down from the ordinary, the mundane, the "serious." So, for example, in Chaucer's *The Parlement of Foules,* we read:

> And in a privee corner, in disporte,
> Fond I Venus and her porter Richesse,

and, in The Wife of Bath's Prologue:

> He hadde a book that gladly nyght and day
> For his disport he wolde rede alway.

Three hundred years later Milton uses the word similarly when he writes, in *Paradise Lost,* of Adam and Eve's fatal dalliance:

> There they thir fill of Love and Love's disport
> Took largely.

And the word *sport* is used with no apparent difference in meaning, for example, in the King James translation of Proverbs 10.23, "It is as sport to a fool to do mischief," and of Judges 16.25, "And it came to pass, when their hearts were merry, that they said, Call for Samson, that he may make us sport. And they called for Samson out of the prison house; and he made them sport; and they set him between the pillars." Thus the word *sport* is, from the time of its earliest appearance, a word of very general application; it can be used to refer to hunting and fishing (Izaak Walton speaks of "this day's sport"), athletic activities, wanton merrymaking, and even erotic foreplay, by-play and interplay.

But it is only in relatively recent times, say in the past two hundred years, that *sport* has been limited to the use to which we now put it.

---

1. See further N. Grell, *Zur Geschichte des Begriffs "Sport" in England und Deutschland,* diss. (Vienna, 1943); J. Sofer, "Kurze Bemerkungen zur Vorgeschichte des Wortes 'Sport,'" *Leibesübungen—Leibeserziehung* 14 (1960) 13–14; E. Mehl, "'Sport' kommt nicht von dis-portare, sondern von de-portare," *Die Leibeserziehung* 15 (1966) 232–33. I am grateful to the University of California Press's anonymous referee for supplying me with copies of the articles by Sofer and Mehl.

Even today we are still likely, it is true, to refer gleefully to the baiting of a particularly gullible colleague as "great sport." And the word occasionally retains some of its earlier associations when we hear of someone doing something "in sport" or when we speak of ourselves as a "sport of circumstances." But these are fossils. It is no longer common, as it once was, to speak of an amorous encounter as "sport." We no longer use *sport,* as Shakespeare did, to refer to theatrical performances. Nowadays we speak of a "play on words" not, as formerly, a "sport of words." We reserve *sport* to distinguish hunting, skiing and football from such diversions as backgammon, gin rummy and crossword puzzles, all of which would at one time have fallen under the rubric "sport." It is this "modern" use of the word—which I have steadfastly resisted defining—that has so seduced the speakers of countless languages throughout the world that they have made the English word, along with its field of reference, their own. One might readily infer from this state of affairs that whatever it is that we now refer to by the name "sport" did not exist anywhere before about the beginning of the eighteenth century and, further, when it did first put in its appearance, it did so among English-speaking people. This would account for the absence of any equivalent to the modern term *sport* in any language, including English, before the eighteenth century. (I can assert on the basis of intimate acquaintance that there is no equivalent in ancient Greek, despite the acknowledged importance of the Greeks in the history of sport, or in Latin.) This would also account for the wide dissemination of the English word and its acceptance into the vocabulary of other languages.

And in fact it is commonly held today that what we think of as sport is precisely an English development of the time of the so-called Industrial Revolution. This view is argued by, among others, Allen Guttmann and Richard Mandell, the authors of two of the most stimulating recent books in English on the history of sport. In *From Ritual to Record,* the former states:

> Modern sport, a ubiquitous and unique form of nonutilitarian physical contests, took shape over a period of approximately 150 years, from the early eighteenth to the late nineteenth centuries. Speaking historically, we can be reasonably precise about place as well as time. Modern sports were born in England and spread from their birthplace to the United States, to Western Europe, and to the world beyond.[2]

---

2. Guttmann, *From Ritual to Record* 57.

Mandell, in his recent book *Sport: A Cultural History,* writes to similar effect:

> During this period [the seventeenth and eighteenth centuries] Englishmen made decisive and influential innovations in social and economic organization and in politics as well. Not uncoincidentally, many Englishmen also began to examine, reject, and refine forms of play or recreation which had been common in comparable social classes all over Europe. In England there evolved some new and broadly based attitudes toward games and competitions and athletes and their performances. These new notions favoring equal (sporting) opportunity, fair play, codified rules, training, transregional leagues, and referees had striking analogues in English social and economic life, which were being transformed. Few historians have noticed that modern sport has characteristics that are distinctive and that modern sport has its origins in precisely those social circumstances that fostered rationalized industrial production. For a while, industrial production and modern sport were uniquely regnant in England and both, subsequently, have spread over much of the world.[3]

It would appear, then, that two different approaches, the historical approach of Guttmann and Mandell and the linguistic approach, combine to produce the same conclusion, and that these different perspectives serve to confirm the validity of that conclusion, namely that modern sport is a wholly novel phenomenon and that it was a product of England at the time of the Industrial Revolution.

Now these scholars, along with a number of other serious historians of sport, have done a great service by focusing attention on the special characteristics of modern sport. But a number of questions still remain. It is not my intention to subject the work of Guttmann, Mandell and others to an extended and rigorous critique. If the thesis to be propounded below, namely that there is no essential difference between modern sport and the sport of other and earlier societies, can be shown to be correct, then such a critique would seem to be unnecessary. After all, once I have constructed a new and wholly satisfactory stable, there will be no need for me to clean out that of Augeas as well. If, on the other hand, my own argument proves to be nothing other than a crock of self-evident nonsense, I would prefer that this essay be consigned to the waves of oblivion rather than be recalled as an eccentric curiosity that happened to contain a meticulous examination of the work of oth-

3. Mandell, *Sport* xv.

ers. Nevertheless, a word must be said about the propriety in general of making statements of the sort, "We (in this time, in this country, in this movement) are unique." The value of studying the ideas, the activities and the beliefs of people who do not belong to our time, our society or our institutions is that it serves to combat provinciality. There is a natural tendency on the part of people to believe that what they do is, in the first place, different from and, in the second place, better than what is done by others. For example, when we look at a society (which we tend to stigmatize as "primitive") that adheres to the practice of painting, tattooing or otherwise decorating the bodies of its members, we tend to react with a feeling of superiority on the grounds that we have transcended such savage customs. When it is pointed out that members of our own society are similarly given to the habit of applying cosmetics to eyes, lips and cheeks (not to mention such uncomfortable and sometimes dangerous innovations as plastic surgery, electrolysis and "tanning salons"), the reaction is typically, "Oh, but that is different." We wish to believe that what we do is done for aesthetic reasons, and we recoil in horror at the suggestion that a woman having her ears pierced in Scarsdale is engaged in precisely the same activity as her counterpart in Tanzania. What lies behind our reaction is the unspoken assumption that the benighted denizens of other times and other places have nothing better to do with their time than to make themselves uglier, while we have progressed to such a level of civility that we have devised methods of improving on nature itself. Even when we criticize our own society, we rarely go beyond such sentiments as, "We are behaving no better than barbarians," or, "This piece of legislation looks as though it belonged in the Middle Ages," thus confirming by implication what we appeared to deny, namely, that "we" are, on the whole, superior to "them." But if it is the case that the human inhabitants of six continents independently developed the custom of applying colorful substances to the face, there ought to be a strong presumption that we are dealing in each instance with the same phenomenon, and it is a matter of some interest to inquire into the causes of the phenomenon. The last thing we want to do is to ask the woman from Scarsdale why she wears lipstick or has her ears pierced. She can only give us an answer in terms of the prejudices and presuppositions of her own society, and it is precisely those prejudices and presuppositions that stand in the way of our understanding what appears to be a widespread phenomenon.

And so when we examine the phenomenon of sport, if it is the case that the human inhabitants of six continents independently developed the practice of engaging in wrestling contests, there ought to be a strong presumption that we are dealing in each instance with the same phenomenon, and it will be my concern to inquire into the causes of the phenomenon. The last thing I shall do is to ask the next person I see engaging in wrestling why he is doing what he is doing. For he will not be able to tell me what I want to know. He may tell me, for instance, that he wrestles because he enjoys it. But this is (presumably) the same answer he would have given had I asked him why he engages in sexual activity, and we are well aware that there are specific biological and physiological considerations that render "enjoyment" only a very partial explanation. Or he may tell me that he wrestles because the university that he attends will not charge him for his education if he does so. But this is to answer my question solely in terms of the values of the society of which our wrestler is a member. For I shall then be curious to find out why this particular society values education so highly that it charges dearly for it and yet exempts some students from the obligation to pay on the basis of criteria that appear to have nothing to do with the goals of education. And in any case, no matter how much I am able to discover about the peculiarities of this strange society, my knowledge will make me no better able to understand why this young man engages in the same activity engaged in by young men in societies that know nothing of universities and athletic scholarships. Finally, he may tell me that he wrestles because he wishes to keep physically fit, or because he cherishes the social atmosphere of the gymnasium, or because he is convinced that his girlfriend will be terribly impressed with him. But all of these can only be partial explanations. Human behavior is inordinately complex, and it is foolish to imagine that any instance of behavior above the level of the reflex can be accounted for simply as the result of a single cause. I cannot give a fully reasoned account of why I chose to wear a blue rather than a grey tie today, much less why I chose to marry Karen rather than Brigitte. Of course it is reasonable to expect that one person will be guided by a variety of causes, that he will join a tennis club for reasons of health *and* because he enjoys the sport *and* in hopes of advancing his career within the corporation for which he works. But, again, even if it were possible to account exhaustively for the motivation of an individual, we would learn only about that individual and, perhaps, about others of his nationality, age or social class. What we are concerned with is rather sport in general, and to this inquiry the question of individual motivation is of doubtful relevance. We may admire the sentiments (although not, perhaps, their manner of expression) of Howard Slusher, whose approach is existential and phenomenological:

> A basic dilemma is one of *causality*. Does man run because of
> *cause* or does he just run? Does he say first, I need to run? I
> need fitness? I need exercise? I need release of tension? I need
> to involve myself with nature? I need a social relationship? It is
> here I must agree with Sartre. Man runs! Cause might or might
> not be present. The importance has been traditionally rested on
> *motivation*. Perhaps it is now time to become *aware* of the hu-
> man element in sport. Motivation is important. But it is time
> we asked what *is* happening when man runs.[4]

What the author of these breathless sentences fails to consider is that
while *individual* motivation may be a matter of little concern, we cannot
very well dispense entirely with considerations of cause if we want to
inquire into the nature of sport in general. It may well be that an individual participates in a sport for reasons that have little or nothing to
do with the essence of sport. (At this point I ought to give an example
of what I mean, but any example would have the effect of pre-judging
what is in fact the essence of sport.) But sport is so nearly a universal
component of human existence that it is reasonable to seek after its
cause or causes.

Why does man engage in sport? The answer to this question, that is
to say, a theory of sport, must satisfy three requirements to be successful
and convincing. In the first place, it must seek to explain the origin of
sport. It is not sufficient to inquire into the origin of basketball. What
is necessary if we are to understand sport is to discover why humans
have always engaged in activities involving running, throwing, rules and
teams. Nor is it legitimate, as we have seen, to assert that somehow
basketball is essentially different from other activities that others have
engaged in that involve running, throwing, rules and teams. For to do
this is to exhibit provincialism and to make value judgments of a sort
that is inappropriate in a scholarly inquiry. For example, one of the
seven characteristics that Guttmann singles out as distinguishing modern sport from sport as practiced in earlier societies is "secularism." Nor
is Guttmann alone, for it is widely believed that the secularization of
sport is an indication that modern sport is fundamentally different from
other manifestations of sport. But to assert this is to make some rather
bold and unwarranted assumptions. In the first place, it is to assume
that the connection between sport and religion in other and earlier so-

---

4. H. Slusher, *Man, Sport and Existence: A Critical Analysis* (Philadelphia, 1967) 54.
All emphasis is, characteristically, Mr. Slusher's.

cieties is fundamental. Indeed, Guttmann makes this assumption, as is made clear when he says:

> For the Jicarilla Apache running between the circles of the sun and the moon or the Athenian youth racing in the stadium built above the sacred way at Delphi, the contest was in itself a religious act. For most contemporary athletes, even for those who ask for divine assistance in the game, the contest is a secular event.[5]

This is precisely analogous to the assertion that, while the members of such-and-such a tribe mutilate their faces because such behavior is an essential part of their rites of initiation, women in our society pierce their ears to make themselves more attractive. In the second place, to assert that secularization marks a fundamental change in modern sport is to assume that earlier there was *always* a connection between religion and sport. But we have no way of knowing the relative ages of sport and religion in human history. It is possible, for example, that sport was in existence long before man developed religious practices, in which case it may be that the connection between sport and religion during some stage of human development is only a secondary (and apparently temporary) phenomenon. Perhaps it is the Apache and the ancient Greek who are unique, not we.

The second requirement that a successful theory of sport must satisfy is that it must be able to account for the persistence of a particular sport within a particular society through various stages of the society's development. For it is clear that sport is remarkably conservative, and many of the sports that we engage in now were also practiced by our very distant ancestors. Nor is it sufficient merely to acknowledge the conservatism of sport. If we are to understand the essence of sport, we must also be able to account for its conservatism. It is perfectly reasonable to account for the origin of the javelin throw in terms of practicing and developing skills necessary for success in hunting and warfare in societies in which hunting and warfare are carried out by means of the manual projection of pointed shafts. But we need also to be able to account for the existence of international competitions in javelin throwing in societies that have relegated hunting itself to the status of a sport and that rely for the killing of their human foe upon the percussive qualities of various chemical and sub-atomic substances. Why should a man who earns his livelihood by spending his days depressing plastic

---

5. Guttmann, *From Ritual to Record* 25.

keys at a computer terminal train his body to be able to throw a javelin farther than it was thrown by those whose very lives depended upon their skill with this weapon?

The first two requirements of a theory of sport, that it explain the origin of sport and that it account for the persistence of specific sports, are of a historical nature and involve a diachronic perspective. The third requirement is of a synchronic nature and demands the skills, not of a historian, but of a philosopher and a lexicographer. It is that a theory of sport must account for the apparent diversity of the activities subsumed under the category "sport." In other words, what is the common element that allows us to apply the one word to such activities as golf, football, weightlifting and mountain climbing? This is a particularly difficult kind of question to answer, because it is so susceptible to the introduction of the vocabulary of valuation. Any attempt at a definition involves some degree of circularity: one cannot define a class until one knows which items belong in the class and which do not, but at the same time one cannot tell whether an item belongs in the class until one knows the characteristics of the class. The difficulties involved in devising a definition are frequently mitigated by the liberal application of personal prejudice. If one is attempting a definition of sport and is oneself a sportsman—as so many who have written about sport proclaim themselves to be—one tends to eliminate from consideration activites (which "others," perhaps, may regard as sport) that are somehow distasteful, inelegant or otherwise unworthy of inclusion in the company of such noble activities as those one practices oneself. For example, H. A. Harris declines to treat gladiatorial combats, the second most popular sport of ancient Rome, in his book *Sport in Greece and Rome*. That this represents a value judgment on the part of the author rather than an oversight is clear from an offhand comment that he makes when he says that the Romans adopted from the Etruscans "gladiatorial and wild beast shows—if these can be called sport."[6] A similar prejudice is exhibited by the other great English historian of ancient sport, E. Norman Gardiner, who describes the evil results of professionalism in ancient Greek sport in terms of what Gardiner perceived to be a parallel phenomenon in his own day:

> The evil effects of professionalism are worst in those fighting events, boxing, wrestling and the pankration, where the feeling of aidōs or honour is most essential. Here again the history of

6. Harris, *Sport* 50.

> modern sport tells the same tale. Wrestling which was once a national sport in England has been killed by professionalism. Amateur boxing is of modern date and owes its existence to the encouragement it receives from the Army and Navy, the Universities, and the Public Schools, but it is overshadowed by professional boxing, and the amateur is continually tempted to turn professional by the enormous sums that he can earn as a public entertainer. . . . When a boxer will not fight unless he is guaranteed a huge purse whether he wins or loses he forfeits all claim to be called a sportsman.[7]

Notice how blatantly Gardiner speaks of Greek sport in terms of the values of his own day, notwithstanding the specious and inappropriate introduction of a genuine ancient Greek word (*aidōs*). And notice the ringing conclusion to the paragraph, which ends on the emotional value-word *sportsman*.

The attitude of Gardiner and Harris is characteristic of the nineteenth- and twentieth-century British view of sport. We ought therefore to be very wary of defining sport in nineteenth- and twentieth-century British terms, and in particular of viewing "sport" as a characteristically modern British development. For when we do this we run the risk of assuming that the features that distinguish sport as we know it from other claimants to the name are somehow the essential features. When we are confronted with a society that engages in sports that have characteristics very different from those of the sports with which we are most familiar, we react by remarking the difference and, sometimes, by questioning whether the other society's sports really deserve the name. This second reaction is exemplified by, among others, Harris' reluctance to vouchsafe the appellation *sport* to so brutal a spectacle as gladiatorial combats; the first is implicit in the description of the Dodo's answer to Alice's question, "What *is* a Caucus-race?"

> First it marked out a race-course, in a sort of circle, ("the exact shape doesn't matter," it said) and then all the party were placed along the course, here and there. There was no "One, two, three, and away!" but they began running when they liked, and left off when they liked, so that it was not easy to know when the race was over. However, when they had been running half an hour or so, and were quite dry again, the Dodo suddenly called out, "The race is over!" and they all crowded round it, panting, and asking, "But who has won?"

7. Gardiner, *Athletics of the Ancient World* 105.

This, of course, is Wonderland, where everything contravenes the dictates of good sense and reason, according to which the exact shape of a racecourse matters greatly, the contestants in a footrace must start at the same time and from the same place, the end of the race is the reason for its having been run and the decisive question about the race is, "Who has won?" Good sense and reason can only be disconcerted by the Dodo's declaration that "*Everybody* has won, and *all* must have prizes." But the caucus-race and, to an even greater extent, the Queen's croquet ground are *meant* to be absurd and disconcerting, at least to the sensibilities of the Victorian British. And so the condign punishment of the most heinous criminal, the profaner of good sportsmanship, is reserved for last in the Mikado's utopia:

> The billiard sharp whom anyone catches,
>   His doom's extremely hard—
>   He's made to dwell—
>   In a dungeon cell
>   On a spot that's always barred.
> And there he plays extravagant matches
>   In fitless finger-stalls
>   On a cloth untrue,
>   With a twisted cue
>   And eliptical billiard balls!

That the Victorian psyche was anxious about the possible existence of billiard tables and croquet grounds with ridges and furrows may tell us a great deal about the Victorians and, perhaps, about Victorian sport, but must not be allowed to dictate to us standards regarding sport tout court. We must be prepared to accept the fact that there are, and have been, societies of people who regard the standards that we consider to be decisive in connection with sport of little or no importance. Even the Dodo's caucus-race can be paralleled. Morris Edward Opler describes an American Indian ritual race that was revived after a period of neglect at the instigation, curiously enough, of four large birds:

> When the last two old men pass the rocks at the west end the two young runners start off as fast as they can. . . . When these first two runners pass the rocks, the second man on each side starts off. Any one of the boys who are painted can take a turn running for his side now. The runners do not have to take part in any certain order after the first two on each side have had their turns. If it is behind, a side will put its best man in and

catch up. Some boys run four or five times, some just once.
There does not have to be the same number of runners on each
side.[8]

Despite the reference to being behind and catching up, it is clear from
the rest of Opler's account that victory in this race is of as little conse-
quence as victory in the race held on the shore of the Pool of Tears in
Alice in Wonderland. For all participants obtain equal benefits from
running in this race: "Boys, even though they are not good runners,
are supposed to run at least once in a race like this. Otherwise they
will always be sickly and poor, for the boys are blessed and helped by
this ceremony." Indeed, there are times when neither side wins. "When
they are even, as they were last year, it means that the fruit and the meat
will be just about the same." For one "side" represents the interests of
the food animals and the other side the interests of vegetation, and
the victory of one side or the other ensures that, for the ensuing
year, the supplies of meat will be greater than those of fruits and vege-
tables or vice versa. But in either case, adequate supplies of food are
guaranteed by the mere fact that the race has been run. Everybody has
won, and all must have prizes.

Now, either we must regard the kind of race that Opler describes as
having a nature wholly different from that of the races run, say, at the
Olympic Games, or we must recognize that, for example, insistence
upon the determination of a winner or upon equal tasks for all participants is not a decisive or necessary characteristic of sport. There are
many, of course, who would deny that there is any connection between
this Indian ritual and a race at an international competition on the
grounds that the one is part of a religious ceremony and the other is an
activity designed to determine the fastest runner over a certain distance
in highly controlled circumstances. But our task is not to pre-judge on
the basis of apparent or alleged motivations, or on the basis of criteria
that are of importance to one society but may turn out upon investigation to be of only superficial application. Rather our task is to cast our
net as widely as possible and then to see if a single explanation can be
found to account for the origin and persistence of such activities as
bullfighting and waterskiing. If we can find such an explanation, we
shall be fairly confident that we have identified the essence and nature
of sport.

8. "The Jicarilla Apache Ceremonial Relay Race," *American Anthropologist* 46 (1944)
90–91. The quotations below are from 75, 78.

Needless to say, this will not be the first attempt at a theory of sport. In fact, the bibliography of previous efforts is enormous. To include a survey of earlier work would double the length of this essay and would not, I am convinced, enhance its value. The reader is referred to the valuable summary, with brief critical remarks, by Hans Lenk, to Christoph Ulf's shorter but more recent contribution to Ingomar Weiler's *Der Sport bei den Völkern der alten Welt,* and to the first section of Horst Ueberhorst's *Geschichte der Leibesübungen.*[9] For convenience and in the interests of brevity, we can, with Ueberhorst, divide the various attempts to explain the origin of sport into three basic approaches. The first is the orthodox Marxist view, according to which physical exercise is an outgrowth of the process of labor and production. The second is an approach based upon the relatively new science of ethology, according to which sports are a manifestation of instinctive drives or impulses. The third view is proclaimed in the opening sentence of Carl Diem's great book, which begins, "Alle Leibesübung war ursprünglich kultisch." If we subject each of these three approaches to scrutiny and apply to them the three requirements that we earlier demanded of a convincing theory of sport, it will be seen that each of the three is, on its own and as it is promulgated by its supporters, inadequate.

Let us begin with the Marxist view, which, on the basis of the number of its adherents, must be regarded as the predominant theory of sport. This theory is set out and elaborated in a great many publications, including the work of Walter Sieger, Gerhard Lukas and Wolfgang Eichel, and the work of many others who contribute to the pages of *Theorie und Praxis der Körperkultur,* the theoretical organ of the Staatliches Komitee für Körperkultur und Sport der DDR.[10] The reader who cannot read German, or who cannot read the ponderous and jargon-filled German in which most Marxist discussions of sport are written, can satisfy himself by reading the ponderous and jargon-filled English article by N. I. Ponomarev or the criticism of the Marxist

9. H. Lenk, "Perspectives of the Philosophy of Sport," in *Scientific View of Sport,* ed. Grupe et al., 31–58; C. Ulf, "Sport bei den Naturvölkern," in Weiler, *Der Sport* 14–52, especially 14–19 and 38–44; H. Ueberhorst, "Ursprungstheorien," in *Geschichte,* ed. Ueberhorst, I 11–38, with English summary, "Theories of Origin" 39–47.

10. W. Sieger, "Die sozialistische Körperkultur als historisch neue Qualität," in *Körperkultur und Sport in der DDR,* ed. G. Wonneberger (Berlin, 1982) 14–73; G. Lukas, *Die Körperkultur in frühen Epochen der Menschheitsentwicklung* (Berlin, 1969); W. Eichel, "Die Entwicklung der Körperübungen in der Urgemeinschaft," *Theorie und Praxis der Körperkultur* 2 (1953) 14–33.

view of sport in Guttmann's *From Ritual to Record*.[11] According to this view, sport arises in early societies as practice for work. Primitive hunters, in order to be successful and productive members of society, needed to be proficient in the use of those tools—bow and arrow, spear, boomerang—that mark man out from his fellow animals, and needed to develop those physical attributes—endurance, speed of foot, ability to swim—that are conducive to survival. Now, on the surface, this appears to be a perfectly rational explanation for the origin of sport: Palaeolithic man recognized that he would be a better hunter if he were more adept at throwing the javelin and if he were swifter afoot, hence physical exercises, competitions and so on. There is, of course, no evidence to prove this theory (and none to disprove it), and we may regard it as an attractive, but unverifiable, hypothesis. While Marxist theory may account adequately for the origins of sport, it has difficulty meeting the other requirements we have laid down. It cannot explain, for example, why javelin throwing persists as a sport in society in which skill in throwing is no longer relevant to the means of production. The best it can do is to speak in terms of general health and physical conditioning, which does not account specifically for javelin throwing as opposed to, say, jogging, and which abandons the Marxist principle that reduces everything to considerations of labor; for surely a desire for health is the one thing that cannot be explained in terms of its relationship to something else, if we are to believe those philosophers from Plato to the present day who use health as the example of that which is pursued for its own sake. Nor can it account for the development of golf; for the skill involved in hitting a small ball with a club into a hole in the ground an eighth of a mile away can hardly have been relevant to the means of production at any time. Presumably the Marxist will regard golf as "bourgeois" and degenerate, but this is to substitute value terms for terms of analysis. A theory of sport must account for golf as well as for footraces, and it is not entitled to question the status of the one or the other on a priori grounds.

Proponents of a theory of sport based upon the findings of the science of ethology are as scarce as the supporters of the Marxist view are legion. The reason for this is that while ethology is eminently well suited to explain the origin of "play" in humans, it cannot account (or

11. N. I. Ponomarev, "Some Research Problems of Physical Education in the Early History of Mankind," *History of Physical Education and Sport: Research and Studies* 2 (1974) 27–45; Guttmann, *From Ritual to Record* 57–89. See also Guttmann's introduction to his translation of B. Rigauer, *Sport and Work* (New York, 1981) vii–xxxi.

has not yet accounted) for the origin of "sport." For no one, regardless of his definition of sport, considers play and sport to be identical. Play is something that humans share with other animals, and there is every reason to believe that play in humans springs from the same source as play among our fellow creatures, namely, a specific impulse to play. Play thus serves a biological function in that it enables the organism to learn from interacting with its environment and from experimenting with the capabilities of its own body. But sport is an exclusively human phenomenon, and it is precisely the differences between humans and other animals that ethology has the greatest difficulty in explaining on its own terms. Konrad Lorenz and Klaus Wiemann explain sport as a form of the (necessary) discharge of intraspecific aggression.[12] But not all sport is aggressive, or even competitive. And in any case it is questionable whether sport has in fact "discharged" more aggression than it has provoked. The Nika Riots in A.D. 532, in the course of which over thirty thousand people were killed, began in the hippodrome in Constantinople. And the hostility aroused by soccer matches in our own time is notorious. As we shall see later, however, the ethologists have failed to recognize the value of their science in explaining the diversity of activities that comprise sport and in accounting for the persistence of particular sports.

Needless to say, the third approach to a theory of sport, namely that according to which sport has cultic origins, holds no interest for the ethologists and is positively anathema to the Marxists, for whom sport is a wholly rational activity that involves the mind as fully as the body, and for whom religious ritual is the embodiment of irrational superstition. To the Marxist, sport and ritual are diametrically opposed to each other as the pragmatic and the magical approaches respectively to success in the struggle against the hostile forces of nature that beset primitive man. Both sport and ritual arise out of the need to solve specific problems of labor and production; neither, therefore, can arise out of the other. The orthodox Marxist might also point out that sport flourishes in those socialist societies that have most rigorously cleansed themselves of religious ritual. And this would be a valid observation. For, even if it were granted that sport is of ritual origin, something else would have to be posited and some other theory of sport introduced in

---

12. Lorenz, *On Aggression* 280–82; K. Wiemann, "Die Phylogenese des menschlichen Verhaltens im Hinblick auf die Entwicklung sportlicher Betätigung," in *Geschichte*, ed. Ueberhorst, I 48–61, with English summary 62–63.

order to explain the apparently total divorce of sport from ritual in many societies in which sport is practiced. In other words, a theory of sport based upon the connection between sport and ritual, even if it could satisfactorily account for the origin of sport, would fail to meet the requirement that we established earlier, namely that a theory of sport ought to be able to account for the persistence of sport.

But, in fact, believers in the ritual nature of sport have not satisfactorily accounted even for the origin of sport. In the literature on sport, the words and concepts *ritual, cult* and *religion* tend to be used more or less interchangeably and without definition, and they tend to be used in such a way as to imply that anything that can be ascribed to "ritual origin" is in need of no further explanation. Even trained anthropologists, who ought to be especially immune to the introduction of prejudices and preconceptions based upon their own cultural orientation, have been guilty of this kind of terminological and conceptual imprecision. In her contribution to the 1956 Festschrift for the Vienna School of Ethnology, Käthe Hye-Kerkdal describes a race among the Timbira tribes of Brazil in which the members of two teams take turns carrying a heavy log over distances of several kilometers:

> For these extraordinary physical accomplishments neither the victorious team nor the outstanding runner receives conspicuous recognition. Here too the race does not exist for the purpose of satisfying the ambition of any individual or group. Nevertheless each runner performs to the best of his ability. What is the reason for these great physical performances? The Timbira are aware of no explanation for them. The examples, however, drawn from the field of other Indian cultures confirm the supposition that the log-races as well, rather than serving the purpose of bringing about physical conditioning, might instead represent the performance of a ritual act [*eine sakrale Handlung*].[13]

Hye-Kerkdal's reaction is echoed by Hans Damm, who refers to Hye-Kerkdal's account of these races:

> Yet the most remarkable feature of these curious races was the fact that the victor did not expect to be treated like a hero, nor was scorn heaped upon the losers. The awareness of having performed to the best of one's abilities in this contest from the

---

13. Hye-Kerkdal, "Wettkampfspiel und Dualorganisation" 514.

point of view of strength and endurance entirely overshadowed the question of determining winners and losers.[14]

It will be seen that this is precisely the reaction of Alice to the Dodo's caucus-race. "The most remarkable feature" of these races is exactly that feature wherein they differ from comparable phenomena in our own society. What requires explanation is why the Timbira run these races at all if they are not going to single out the victors for special reward and recognition. The immediate implication, of course, is that the conferment of special rewards and recognitions upon victors is a sufficient explanation for the existence of competitive races. The further implication is that any race that is run for some other reason stands in need of special explanation.

And that explanation is ready to hand. Any phenomenon among primitive folk that is odd, irrational or otherwise difficult to explain can confidently be set down to the requirements of cultic practice. And, to be sure, in the case of sport this kind of explanation is particularly attractive. There is an enormous ethnographical literature, to which Damm, Jensen and Körbs both refer and contribute, which documents the intimate connection among so-called primitive peoples between sports and other activities of a ritual nature. The Hopi Indians of Arizona competed in footraces in which the runners symbolized rain and clouds, the purpose of which was to produce rain. A ritual tug-of-war, also intended to encourage rainfall, has been observed in Laos. The Aztecs engaged in elaborately organized ball-games, the "religious" and cosmic symbolism of which is noted by all commentators.[15] Numerous games and sports in various societies are ascribed to ritual origin on the grounds that the native participants recount myths attributing the invention of the game or sport to some divine or legendary figure. If it were not possible to account on other grounds for the universal human practice of consuming food, it would presumably be possible to explain the phenomenon as a religious practice, inasmuch as countless societies can be found in which there is an intimate association between eating and other ritual activities.

It would appear, therefore, that the theory of sport based upon the notion that sport is of ritual origin has the least to recommend it. In

14. Damm, "Vom Wesen sogenannter Leibesübungen" 5; cf. also Diem, *Weltgeschichte des Sports* 76.
15. Damm, "Vom Wesen sogenannter Leibesübungen" 5 (Hopi), 4 (Laos); Körbs, "Kultische Wurzel" 13 (Aztecs).

the first place, the proponents of this theory have failed to account satisfactorily for the origin of sport. In the second place, demonstration of the ritual origin of sport still leaves us with a need for yet another explanation to account for the persistence of sport outside of ritual contexts. Finally, proponents of this view do not even try to account for the diversity of activities that comprise sport, nor would it be easy to explain the development of golf or body-surfing in terms of the requirements of cult. I should like to show, however, that it is not the inherent weakness of this approach that renders it unsatisfactory as a theory of sport. Rather the failure results from the theoretical and methodological flaws in the work of its supporters. We have already seen that there is a (reprehensible) tendency to regard anything that can be ascribed to ritual origin as not requiring any further explanation. But there is also a tendency, based upon prejudice and conditioned by familiarity with modern sport, to wonder why an activity as seemingly "secular" as sport should be related to ritual. After acknowledging the ritual character of primitive sport, some scholars have been driven to ask, "What is the connection between sport and ritual?" Now, this is certainly a legitimate question. It is not immediately obvious, either to the tribesmen themselves or to the reflective ethnographer, why a tug-of-war between two groups of tribesmen should result in increased rainfall, or why physically enervating footraces held on a regular basis should be counted upon to enhance the fecundity of the population. This question is usually answered with silence, either out of humility or out of an innate sense of superiority (ritual is merely a form of magic, having its own kind of logic, which is inaccessible to the rational mind of the scientific inquirer). But occasionally an answer is expressed—and it is regularly the same, unsatisfactory answer. It was suggested as long ago as 1907 by Stewart Culin, the pioneer among ethnographers of sport. Referring to the almost universal practice of engaging in games and sports, he notes that they are performed not only for the purposes of enjoyment and recreation, but "also as religious ceremonies, as rites pleasing to the gods."[16] In an entirely different connection, and independently of Culin, H. A. Harris writes, "The Greeks were strongly anthropomorphic in their conception of their deities, and assumed that what gave pleasure to themselves—music, drama or sport—would equally be gratifying to the gods."[17] And, similarly, Michael A. Salter,

16. Culin, *Games of the North American Indians* 809.
17. Harris, *Sport* 16.

in discussing the deities worshipped by the Indians of the eastern woodlands of North America, says, "In most cases the entities involved were believed to be like their worshippers, passionately fond of games."[18] This is a satisfyingly rational explanation, and its widespread acceptance indicates that it has satisfied many. But what is rational can as well be a rationalization as a reason. And this explanation deserves to be regarded as having the same status as the (equally rationalizing) myths put forward by the participants themselves to account for the origin of individual games.

In case it still needs to be said, I should like to point out that it is arguing in a circle to assert both that men engage in sports because they believe that by doing so they are pleasing the gods and that sport is pleasing to the gods because the gods are fond of that which is pleasing to men. A similar circularity afflicts the discussion of the relationship between sports and funeral rites. Gardiner writes that in ancient Greece, sports "were appropriate at funeral games where they might be supposed to be pleasing to the spirit of the deceased who had in his lifetime found his pleasure therein."[19] This idea is at least as old as Virgil, who writes:

> The pleasure those heroes had felt,
> When alive, in their arms and chariots, the care they had taken to pasture
> Their sleek horses—all was the same beyond the tomb.

Indeed, of the spirits of the dead in Virgil's underworld,

> Some exercise upon the grassy playing-fields
> Or wrestle on the yellow sands in rivalry of sport.[20]

But the belief that the dead take pleasure in the same kind of activities as the living cannot be used as part of an explanation for the origin of sports. In the first place, as noted above, such an argument would be circular. In the second place, there is no reason to believe that the notion of the survival of the spirit of the deceased is any older than the

18. M. A. Salter, "Meteorological Play-Forms of the Eastern Woodlands," *History of Physical Education and Sport: Research and Studies* 3 (1975–76) 12.

19. Gardiner, *Athletics of the Ancient World* 33. Similarly 20 and, concerning the Etruscans, 120.

20. Virgil, *Aeneid* 6. 653–55 and 642–43, trans. C. Day Lewis (Oxford, 1952). Virgil is imitating Pindar (frag. 129. 6 Snell) and is in turn imitated by Milton (*Paradise Lost* 2. 528–32).

development of sports and contests. Indeed, humans probably engaged in sports long before they developed the notion of an afterlife.

Perhaps aware of this, Carl Diem attempts a somewhat more sophisticated explanation of the development of contests from funeral rites. Diem acknowledges that the belief exists among many peoples that funeral games exist for the purpose of pleasing the spirits of the dead. This belief is in keeping with the very widespread custom of leaving offerings of foodstuffs and other material objects at the graves of the deceased. Diem notes that the deceased is conceived of as a fellow spectator at the games held in his honor, and he perceptively compares the existence today of a seat of honor in the Panathenaic Stadium in Athens with the name of Pierre de Coubertin on it. He continues:

> But we may suppose that in the cult of the dead there lies a still deeper meaning than the mere idea that we do not wish to be separated from the dead nor do they wish to be separated from us. . . . Ortega y Gasset believes that primitive man, since death is incomprehensible to him, seeks a culprit. In those instances where it is not obviously a case of murder, the death must have been brought about by telepathic means. He who was suspected of this black magic would be put to death at the grave of the deceased. With the advance of civilization the accused man was at least given the opportunity of exonerating himself by means of an ordeal [*Gottesurteil*]. A duel to the death took the place of an execution. In the next stage of development this bloody contest was transformed into a sporting competition.[21]

But it is questionable method to proceed upon assumptions about the mentality of "primitive man." Furthermore, we see that here too it is necessary to posit a belief in the existence of entities other than and beyond living human beings in whose interest sporting competitions are held. For implicit in the word *ordeal,* and explicit in the German word used both by Diem and Meuli,[22] is the presence of some being or beings ("the gods") who render judgment. Thus we find that those who have attempted to explain the origin of sport in ritual and religious terms are unable to avoid circularity of argument: sport is practiced in the interests of supernatural beings (the gods, the spirits of the dead), and those supernatural beings are interested in sport because they are

21. Diem, *Weltgeschichte des Sports* 30–31. What is attributed by Diem to Ortega should in fact be ascribed to Meuli, "Ursprung" 195–97 (= *Gesammelte Schriften* II 889–91).

22. Meuli, "Ursprung" 197 and 208 (= *Gesammelte Schriften* II 891–92 and 905).

conceived of in strictly human terms. (We may also add that the attempt to explain sport as arising out of funeral combats does not account for non-competitive sports.)

Apart from the various attempts to show that sport has its origins in religious ritual, there have also been numerous studies devoted to examining the relationship between sport and religion in general. There is a useful survey and generous bibliography in Hans Wissmann's contribution to *The Scientific View of Sport*.[23] There can be no doubt that the connections between sport and religion are numerous and well documented. In most societies, sports events are associated with, or form part of, religious festivals. In ancient Greece, all athletic contests, including the Olympic Games, were held in honor of one or another of the gods. And these contests were all celebrated as regularly recurring festivals, the timing of which was carefully determined in accordance with strict observance of ritual propriety. And when the Olympic Games were revived in modern times, they were first held at a time when Western and Orthodox Easters coincided. Nor has it gone with its significance unnoticed that, for example, bullfights and American football matches take place on Sundays. The ritual associations of such sports as sumo wrestling are obvious to all, and, indeed, it is regularly pointed out that sports are among the most highly ritualized activities in modern society. It is even suggested that, in many respects, sport has taken over the rôle that was once played in society by religion. This view has a certain superficial attraction, for the idea that sport has replaced religion seems to reinforce the notion that sport has religious origins. But this is to ignore the fact that sport has flourished and has been as highly ritualized in societies that did not feel the lack of other avenues of religious expression. One thinks of the mediaeval jousts and the chariot races of the Byzantine empire.

The difficulty with all these studies is that they fail, or do not attempt, to show what the essential connection between sport and religion is. It seems somehow churlish to point out that one would expect sports events to take place on Sundays and holidays, simply because those are the days on which people are not otherwise engaged. Nevertheless, this is a legitimate point. The association between sport and holidays in modern society attains its apparent significance only under the influence of the preconceived notion, based upon the frequent co-

23. H. Wissmann, "Sport and Non-Christian Religions," in *Scientific View of Sport*, ed. Grupe et al., 99–103 and 112–15.

incidence of sport and religious festivals in earlier societies, that there is in fact a connection between sport and religion. If the association in our own day can be explained in some other way than by the assumption of a necessary and inherent connection between sport and religion,[24] then it may be the case that in earlier societies as well the connection between the two was only superficial. Therefore it is reasonable to demand that an account be given of the exact relationship between sport and religious ritual. It is obviously inadequate merely to point, as so many ethnographers have done, to the frequent collocation of the two.

To begin with, what is clearly called for is an acceptable definition of *ritual*. For it ought to be obvious that it is not fruitful to define sport in terms of ritual without first having a secure concept of what ritual is. Nevertheless, Carl Diem, for whom "All physical exercise was originally ritual," does not attempt to define the term. Nor does Allen Guttmann indicate, in his book *From Ritual to Record,* what he takes the second word of his title to mean. Both Diem and Guttmann seem to understand by *ritual* something like "the kinds of things that are done in connection with religion." And, since sport is among the things that used to be "done in connection with religion," it must at one time have been a form of ritual. But, even leaving aside the difficulty posed by the fact that we still need some kind of definition of *religion,* this is obviously not rigorous enough to be of any help. In fact, as I hope to show, once we are armed with a satisfactory definition of *ritual,* we shall see that the objections raised earlier to the theory that accounts for sport in terms of ritual are only apparent. We shall then be in a position to understand the nature and the origin of sport.

The first thing we must do is recognize that ritual is not always, or fundamentally, connected with religion. While many human rituals—and those, perhaps, the most conspicuous—are indeed associated with religious practice or were originally of a religious nature, there are also numerous rituals that have no religious associations. A good example in our own society is the ceremony accompanying graduation from college. Indeed many rituals are now to be found associated with athletic contests, like the singing of the national anthem before a game or the lighting of the Olympic torch (which, incidentally, is a modern inven-

---

24. See especially J. Lowerson, "Sport and the Victorian Sunday: The Beginnings of Middle-class Apostasy," *British Journal of Sports History* 1 (1984) 202–20. I owe this reference to Professor J. K. Anderson, who is responsible for several other suggestions and improvements in these essays.

tion and has no precedent in the ancient games). The existence of these rituals is acknowledged even by those who deny that modern sports are themselves in any sense rituals. But if sports among primitive peoples are regarded as ritual activities on the grounds that they are regularly associated with rituals, what is to prevent us from considering modern sports as well, not only as ritualized, but as ritual activities? In fact, given the historical circumstances, one would think that there should be a strong presumption that sport today, as it has always been, is an example of ritual. The reason that this presumption is so frequently and so strongly resisted is the failure on the part of most of those who have written on sport to distinguish between ritual and religion. It is important so to distinguish. Even if sport is in fact a form of ritual activity, as I shall shortly argue, it is not legitimate to assume that, since much ritual activity is religious, sport is a religious activity. Yet it is this assumption, in combination with the conviction that modern sport is "secularized," that has prevented those who have written about sport from recognizing the ritual nature of sport.

Even those who emphasize the original connection between sport and ritual are convinced that sport has now evolved into something entirely different and that it is inappropriate to speak of modern sport in terms of ritual. From the point of view of constructing a theory of sport, this view is particularly unsatisfactory. It begins by assuming that activities like footraces, for example, can be explained as arising out of ritual requirements. This is unsatisfactory in that it does not in fact explain what it purports to explain. Why, one wishes to know, are ritual requirements satisfied by footraces rather than by nail biting? The implication of this view is that the assumption of ritual origins (and, for most writers, this means religious origins) frees one of the obligation to give any more thought to the question of origins. Now, according to this view, sport has ceased to be associated with ritual. Since no explanation was given of why sport should be associated with ritual in the first place, there is surely no need to explain why the association was terminated. Subsequently, sport was engaged in "for its own sake."[25] But of how many activities can it be said that they are engaged in "for their own sake"? And which is the more fraudulent explanation, the one that speaks in terms of ritual origins because it is unable to give a rational account, or the one that asserts that the phenomenon needs no explanation on the grounds that it occurs spontaneously? Even if neither

---

25. Guttmann, *From Ritual to Record* 26; Jensen, *Myth and Cult* 64.

explanation were demonstrably fraudulent, the mere fact that two explanations are necessary would make us suspicious. (Why posit ritual origins for sport and then distinguish between ritual and sport, a distinction that further necessitates an explanation of non-ritual sport?) And our suspicions are even further aroused by this particular combination of explanations. For, if modern sports can be engaged in "for their own sake," what is to prevent us from using the same explanation to account for sport among primitive peoples? And if sport can be engaged in "for its own sake," why did it take mankind such a (presumably) long time to discover that an activity that had been practiced only for external reasons needed no external reasons?

In fact, of course, there are no activities that are practiced for their own sake. There are, however, many activities that humans engage in for reasons of which they are themselves unaware. And many of these activities are, if we use the most satisfactory definition of the term, rituals. In fact, it is precisely characteristic of ritual acts that the actions themselves persist long after the original need in response to which the actions arose has disappeared. Thus it would be perfectly in keeping with the concept of ritual, for example, to regard the javelin throw at the Olympic Games as an instance of ritual. Those who participate in the activity are doing so not because they wish to be, or to appear to be, proficient hunters. Indeed, there is no apparent connection between javelin throwing and hunting in modern society. Rather the participants are throwing the javelin because men in the previous generation threw the javelin, and in the generation before that, and in the generation before that, and so on back to a time when there was in fact a connection between javelin throwing and hunting. Earlier, mention was made of the ritual associated with graduation from college. When I ask my students why they are going to dress up in odd robes and funny hats, take part in a procession, and listen to insipid music and interminable speeches at the end of their term of studies, they are unable to give any more satisfactory answer than, "Because I wouldn't feel as though I had really graduated otherwise," or "Because graduation is always like that," or "Because my parents want to see me go through the same kind of ceremony that they went through." Even my colleagues, who preside over this annual ritual, are for the most part ignorant of the connection between hats, robes and processions on the one hand and the conferment of the baccalaureate on the other. And why the participants in the ritual should be designated "bachelors" at the end of it is a mystery to all.

Nor is this the only ritual activity that people are in the habit of performing. There are countless rituals that are familiar to all, and it is characteristic of them that those who perform them are either unable to give any explanation at all for their behavior or give an explanation that is demonstrably inadequate to account for the origin of the behavior. It is traditional, for example, in many Christian countries to accompany the celebration of Easter with a ritual that involves painting, or otherwise adorning, birds' eggs. If one of those participating in this ritual is asked why he does this, his answer is likely to be merely that this activity is a traditional feature of the Easter celebration. When asked why this should be a traditional feature of the celebration of the anniversary of Christ's passion, he may, if he is perceptive enough to recognize that decorating eggs is an obvious element of fertility magic, reply that the activity is symbolic either of the eternal life conferred by Christ's sacrifice or of the resurrection of Christ that Easter celebrates. But this too is characteristic of ritual, that an action that originated for one purpose should continue to be performed for an apparently different purpose. The important point here is that a practice that was once intended to bring about fecundity by magical means at the time of the vernal equinox persists even in a society that employs chemical fertilizers to enhance the fecundity of its fields and of its women, and even in connection with the celebration of a festival characteristic of a religion that, most of its adherents would assert, is totally divorced from magical practice. And just as most Christians would deny that their practice of coloring Easter eggs has anything to do with the magical practices of pagan antiquity, so most (indeed, perhaps all) athletes today would deny that the footraces in which they compete have any connection with races run by primitive peoples for the purpose of encouraging rainfall or improving the fertility of crops.

Another tradition connected with Easter that has no direct relevance to the dogma of Christianity or the circumstances that Easter celebrates is that of the Easter hare, which is, according to the evidence assembled by Charles J. Billson, variously called upon to provide sport, food or an explanation for the presence of the colored eggs. For there are records of Easter hare hunts and of Easter meals consisting of hare in seventeenth- and eighteenth-century England, and "the children in South Germany are told that a hare lays the Pasche eggs, and a nest is made for the hare to lay them in."[26] Even today children are given Easter baskets in which are what appear to be nests filled with eggs (either

---

26. C. J. Billson, "The Easter Hare," *Folk-Lore* 3 (1892) 441–66; cf. also *Das Kloster* 7 (1847) 928; *Schweizerisches Archiv für Volkskunde* 1 (1897) 115.

real or made of candy) and candy rabbits. A more palpable fertility rite is difficult to conceive, and the elements of it long antedate the advent of Christianity. And yet it no longer exists for the purpose of enhancing fertility. Why, then, does the practice persist? Well, because it is traditional. And the same explanation can be given for the persistence of other elements of Christian (and, presumably, other) celebrations. Even in Hawaii, for instance, Christians go to great expense to import evergreens at Christmastime, so that they can engage in a ritual that also has obvious origins in pagan vegetation magic. Another ritual associated with Christmas is that of giving gifts, which is explained (if it is explained at all) as a commemoration of the gifts brought by the "Three Wise Men" at the time of Christ's nativity. But, apart from the fact that the gift-giving engaged in by modern celebrants is of an entirely different nature from that engaged in by the Wise Men, it is well known that the practice of exchanging gifts at this time of the year antedates the birth of Christ. Gift-giving was a prominent feature of the Republican festival of the Saturnalia at Rome, a festival that began on 17 December and lasted for as many as seven days. Among the presents commonly given were wax candles and ceramic dolls to children. This festival was held in honor of the god Saturn, who was felt to have presided over a "golden age." (In his famous fourth Eclogue, written in 40 B.C., Virgil predicts that the Saturnian golden age will shortly return, for which reason he was credited by many early Christian writers with having correctly foretold the birth of Christ.) While several of the features of the modern celebration of Christmas are survivals from the Saturnalia, the date of the celebration, fixed at 25 December only in the fourth century, was chosen, not because anyone knew on what day Christ had been born, but because there was a wish to associate this celebration with the winter solstice (which fell on this date in the Julian calendar) and with the celebration of the birthday of the god Sol Invictus.[27]

The purpose of this digression has been merely to show that it is not uncommon for people to engage in ritual activities, and that some of these activities, like many sports events, were at one time or another connected with festivals of an agrarian nature. That they are no longer connected with such festivals does not indicate that they are no longer to be considered ritual activities. Indeed, as indicated above, it is char-

---

27. H. Usener, *Das Weihnachtsfest,* second edition (Bonn, 1911); J. G. Frazer, *Adonis, Attis, Osiris: Studies in the History of Oriental Religion* I, third edition (London, 1914) 304–12.

acteristic of rituals that they persist in this way. We have not yet considered the question of origins; at this point it is irrelevant whether the customs of running footraces or of giving gifts at midwinter were "originally" of an agrarian nature. What is relevant to the question of whether they are entitled to be considered "rituals" is the fact that they persist outside the context in which they were once felt to be appropriate. But not all rituals take place in connection with religious observance, and many were never associated with vegetation magic. A common type of ritual is to be found in connection with greetings and leavetakings. When we meet someone we frequently take his right hand in our own. If asked why we do this, we simply say that it is traditional or that it is polite, neither of which is an adequate explanation of the connection between the gesture and the circumstances in which it takes place. Similarly, when we take leave of someone we raise our right hand in the air and wave it about. This too is a ritual, and we are unable to explain why we wave our hand when we say goodbye. If we ask a soldier why he salutes his superior officer, he will reply that it is part of his military code to do so, and that there is a specific punishment awaiting him should he fail to salute. But he may be unable to explain the relationship between the specific gesture of raising the right hand to the forehead and the specific punishment for failure to observe the custom. We, however, can give at least a partial explanation. The raising of hand to forehead is a vestige of the practice of touching the hand to the brim of the hat, a gesture that was common even among civilians at the time when it was customary for men to wear hats. This gesture in turn arose from the habit among mediaeval knights of either removing their helmets or lifting their visors in greeting. What the origin of the practice of uncovering the head or face is cannot be precisely determined, but the fact is that the military salute persists, even though the days of helmets and visors have passed.

This last example was taken from the work of the ethologist Irenäus Eibl-Eibesfeldt,[28] and it is to the science of ethology, which Eibl-Eibesfeldt defines as "the biology of behavior,"[29] that we must turn for a clear and satisfying definition of ritual. Konrad Lorenz, in his classic study *On Aggression,* describes the origin of this understanding of ritual:

28. Eibl-Eibesfeldt, *Love and Hate* 55; cf. D. Morris, *The Naked Ape* (New York, 1967) 163.
29. Eibl-Eibesfeldt, *Ethology* 9.

Shortly before the First World War when my teacher and friend, Sir Julian Huxley, was engaged in his pioneer studies on the courtship behavior of the Great Crested Grebe, he discovered the remarkable fact that certain movement patterns lose, in the course of phylogeny, their original specific function and become purely "symbolic" ceremonies. He called this process ritualization and used this term without quotation marks; in other words, he equated the cultural processes leading to the development of human rites with the phylogenetic processes giving rise to such remarkable "ceremonies" in animals. From a purely functional point of view this equation is justified, even bearing in mind the difference between the cultural and phylogenetic processes.[30]

The most celebrated example of ritualized behavior in the animal world that Lorenz cites is the "triumph ceremony" of the greylag goose. The behavior exhibited in this ceremony originally evolved for the purpose of threatening enemies or potential enemies. But this aggressive behavior has been redirected in such a way as to function as a means of creating a bond between male and female. The male goose directs this aggressive behavior toward a nonexistent (in human terms, "imaginary") enemy in the presence of his mate or prospective mate. This serves the purpose of reassuring the female, as if to show the female that, should danger threaten, he will be equal to the challenge. Lorenz perhaps overemphasizes this particular ritual as a result of his interest in aggressive behavior. There are rituals that arise out of behavior that is not inherently aggressive. But what characterizes this "phylogenetic ritualization" is that an innate behavior pattern takes on a new function.

Analogous to phylogenetic ritualization is cultural ritualization. The only difference between the two is that the ritualized behavior in the latter is not innate. But, since the function of phylogenetic and cultural ritualization is the same, it is legitimate to regard them as essentially the same phenomenon. Lorenz defines ritualization as the process whereby

a behavior pattern by means of which a species [or] . . . a cultured society . . . deals with certain environmental conditions, acquires an entirely new function, that of communication. The primary function may still be performed, but it often recedes

30. Lorenz, *On Aggression* 57–58, referring to J. S. Huxley, "The Courtship-Habits of the Great Crested Grebe (*Podiceps cristatus*); with an Addition to the Theory of Sexual Selection," *Proceedings of the Zoological Society of London* (1914) 491–562.

more and more into the background and may disappear completely so that a typical change of function is achieved.[31]

Lorenz and Eibl-Eibesfeldt describe further characteristics of cultural ritualization, specifically: (1) ritualization frequently serves the further function, through its communicative character, of redirecting aggression; (2) it also serves to promote the formation of bonds between pairs or among larger groups; and (3) the ritualized behavior is typically modified in such a way as to enhance its communicative power. This last is achieved by means of the exaggeration, stylization or repetition of the behavior.[32]

It should by now be obvious that the ethologists' definition of ritual is of great value in the understanding of sport. Specifically, it enables us, as no other approach can, to account for the persistence of specific sports in contexts in which they appear to be inappropriate. Also, the characteristics of ritualized behavior can be seen to coincide remarkably well with those of the activities of sport. We shall in due course examine exactly what it is that sport communicates, but it is clear in any case that many sports have either lost their original function entirely, or have pushed it into the background, and that in some general sense they serve the function of display. Throwing the javelin, for example, had a very specific function in the context of hunting and warfare. Now throwing the javelin persists as a sport, not for its original purpose, namely to kill wild animals or human enemies, but in order to show who can throw the javelin the farthest. And, in general, hunting and fishing originally served a very specific function, namely the providing of food. But in agricultural societies, in which food animals have been domesticated, hunting and fishing are frequently still encountered, again (at least in part) for the purpose of display. What is characteristic of the "big-game hunter" is precisely that he is *not* hunting for the purpose of putting food on his table. It is not that he needs to eat the meat of the lion or the rhinoceros. If he does, indeed, eat some of his prey, that is secondary. His reason for going on the hunt is to prove that he is capable of prevailing over the dread elephant or the fierce moose. The "proof" is the obligatory photograph showing the hero standing triumphantly over his defeated victim, or the "trophy" in the form of tusk or horn or stuffed carcass. The sport fisherman too fishes not (or not primarily) in order to feed himself and his family. Indeed,

31. Lorenz, *On Aggression* 75.
32. Ibid. 75ff.; Eibl-Eibesfeldt, *Love and Hate* 51–56, *Ethology* 112–15.

in many instances the sportsman catches fish only to throw them back. In doing so he proclaims his "sportsmanship." And he proclaims it so loudly and conspicuously that it is obvious that here too we are concerned with an activity that is carried on for the purpose of display. (What he is displaying, by the way, is not his humanitarian compassion for the fish. How can one who enjoys manoeuvring barbs into the mouths of fish and then removing them feel compassion? Rather he is displaying to all those to whom he proclaims his compassion his disdainful superiority to the trout.) Other sports as well tell the same story. Running, jumping, swimming and throwing all served at one time (and, in some contexts, still serve) functions directly related to the success of the individual and the group in interacting with the environment. When these activities are engaged in as sports, whether in primitive societies or in urban industrialized societies, they function as a means of communication or display. When they are engaged in competitively, the victor proclaims that he can throw farther or more accurately, or that he can run farther or faster, than anyone else. When they are not competitive, the participant is still communicating, proclaiming that he can throw this far, or swim this fast.

Let us examine the remaining characteristics of "ritual" to see how well sport fits into the category of ritual as defined by the science of ethology. That sport serves the function of redirecting aggression is a commonplace of the literature on sport, and it is emphasized even by those who have no interest in explaining sport in terms of ritual.[33] In some cases it is quite obvious that a specific sport has arisen out of what were originally aggressive impulses. This is particularly clear in the ritualized forms of combat that are such a conspicuous feature of the sporting life of many societies. One thinks first of such sports as judo and amateur wrestling, in which the rules are specifically designed so as to prevent injury being done to the participants. Even in the more violent sports, such as boxing and ice hockey, some provision is made so that injuries will be less likely to be disabling or fatal. But aggression takes the form not only of physical violence but also of seizing and protecting territory and property, and several sports can be seen to have evolved as ritual enactments of this type of aggressive behavior. One thinks of such activities as tug-of-war, of various ball games the object of which

33. E.g., E. Berry, *The Philosophy of Athletics* (New York, 1927) 14; A. R. Beisser, *The Madness in Sports: Psychosocial Observations on Sports* (New York, 1967) 161, 184–91; G. Vinnai, *Fussballsport als Ideologie* (Frankfurt am Main, 1970) 83–95.

is to keep the ball out of the hands of the opposition, of games (like American football) the object of which is to occupy and extend one's possession of territory. Indeed, Lorenz asserts that "the most important function of sport lies in furnishing a healthy safety valve for that most indispensable and, at the same time, most dangerous form of aggression that I have described as collective militant enthusiasm."[34] And he considers that sport in general originated "in highly ritualized but still serious hostile fighting."[35] While we may disagree with Lorenz's view of the origin of sport—How, for example, can we account for the development of non-aggressive and non-competitive sports?—and while we may not be convinced that the redirection of aggression is "the most important function" of sport, it is clearly one of the features of sport that makes sport a valuable item in the repertory of human activities and that helps to ensure the persistence of sport. In any case, ethology does not insist that all rituals serve the function of redirecting aggression, or even that such rituals as do serve this purpose serve no other. We are merely concerned to show that sport, like ritual generally, often does serve as an outlet for aggression.

The second characteristic of cultural ritualization that we referred to above is that it encourages, indeed is one of the vehicles of, group cohesion. Ritualization brings about group cohesion in a variety of ways, and it can be seen that sport functions similarly. One way in which ritualized behavior encourages cohesion is by promoting bonding between mates. In Lorenz's example, the aggressive behavior of the greylag gander has been ritualized to serve as courtship behavior. The gander "impresses" his mate with his ability to protect her, and she has "confidence" in him and feels secure. A college roommate of mine was a fine tennis player, but he had a rather lethargic attitude. He was the number two player on the college team, and was quite satisfied with his position. It was only at the instigation of his girlfriend that he was inspired to challenge for the number one position. In Homer's *Odyssey* the hero of the poem regains his wife by defeating in an archery contest the suitors who have gathered during his twenty-year absence. Such competitive contests are not uncommon in Greek myth and literature. Odysseus is said to have won Penelope in the first place by defeating the other suitors in a footrace.[36] The hand of Atalanta was won in a

34. Lorenz, *On Aggression* 281.
35. Ibid. 280.
36. Pausanias, *Description of Greece* 3.12.1.

footrace. Pelops earned the right to marry Hippodameia by winning a chariot race against her father.[37] For the ancient Greeks, these were all incidents that belonged in the remote and legendary past. There is evidence, however, that many societies have in fact engaged in ritualized competitions for the purpose of selecting mates. Brides among the Kirghiz and the Calmucks were won by means of races on horseback. Footraces are recorded in various parts of Asia, the object of which is to prove the suitability of the groom. Such races were known in Germany even in the nineteenth century. These and other examples are collected in the fascinating pages of Frazer's *The Magic Art*.[38] This kind of race, of course, is precisely analogous to what we frequently find elsewhere in the animal kingdom. Fights or races among males of a species are common elements of natural selection, ensuring that males that exhibit superior aggressiveness, speed or endurance are more likely to secure a mate and to reproduce.

In social animals, ritualized behavior serves, not only to promote bonding among pairs, but also to define larger groups and cause them to cohere. In many instances this behavior is a form of ritualized collective aggression. Sometimes the aggression is directed against another group. Sometimes, on the other hand, an individual or a smaller group within the larger group is singled out as a "scapegoat," the aggression being directed against him or it.[39] In many other instances, however, the behavior is not aggressive, as in the case of ritualized sacrifice and the communal meal.[40] Also essential for cohesion among social groups is ranking within the group, and many ritualized forms of behavior have evolved for the purpose of clarifying the social hierarchy.[41] It will be readily acknowledged that sport, both in contemporary society and elsewhere, serves the same function as other forms of ritualized behavior. Indeed, sociologists of sport have written extensively on the function of sport in promoting group cohesion and in clarifying social ranking.[42] The group is united by rallying round a team or a totem. Whether the team is regional (as in the case of modern football teams or in the case of the national teams at the Olympic Games) or is based upon some other principle of organization seems to make little difference. The racing fans of ancient Rome divided themselves into supporters of the

37. I. Weiler, *Der Agon im Mythos* (Darmstadt, 1974) 209–17, 256–58.
38. Frazer, *Magic Art* II 300—308.
39. Eibl-Eibesfeldt, *Love and Hate* 164–68.
40. Ibid. 167–68; van der Leeuw, *Religion in Essence and Manifestation* 356–58.
41. Eibl-Eibesfeldt, *Love and Hate* 85–89.
42. See the extensive bibliography in *Handbook of Social Science of Sport,* ed. G. R. F. Lüschen and G. H. Sage (Champaign, Ill., 1981) 565–68 and 593–607.

"Greens" and the "Blues," and the teams that compete in the log races among the Timbira Indians are of different composition on different occasions.[43] And if one witnesses an individual sport, say a tennis match or a boxing match, one is expected to be a supporter of one or another of the contestants. Again, it seems to make little difference whether one declares oneself a supporter of this one or that one. Even the criteria by which one chooses one's champion are irrelevant. What matters is the fact that the ritual is performed and witnessed. Socialization is promoted in two ways. The individual, whether he has participated on a team or has merely identified himself as a fan of one side or the other, secures an identity as part of a group. The group manifests its commitment to ranking by declaring winners and losers.

The third characteristic of ritualized behavior that we referred to above is that such behavior tends toward exaggeration, stylization and repetition. Lorenz and Eibl-Eibesfeldt cite as examples the exaggerated movements that characterize military marches and academic processions, and the stylized forms of utterance that one encounters in religious ceremony.[44] These features are also characteristic of all forms of dance, the relationship of which to sport is very close and problematic. They are also clearly characteristic of sport itself. The long jumper or the high jumper does not merely jump. He jumps as far or as high as he possibly can. The discus thrower does not merely throw. He is intent upon throwing to the utmost of his ability. The movements of the diver and the gymnast are stylized to the point of caricature. Indeed their performance is judged on the basis of the degree of stylization that they exhibit. Sports events are repeated, not only in primitive societies, but also in modern Western society, to the point where they serve, as other rituals do, to define and mark the passing of time. The season for the Turkish tournament known as *djerid* opened at the beginning of spring.[45] The ancient Olympic Games were held with meticulous regularity every four years, at the time of the second full moon after the summer solstice.[46] Bullfights in Spain take place on Sundays, the season lasting from Easter to October.

We have shown, then, that the ethological definition of ritual defines sport as well, and that the characteristics of ritual are also the characteristics of sport. At the very least, it should by now be clear that this is

---

43. Nimuendajú, *Eastern Timbira* 140.
44. Lorenz, *On Aggression* 76; Eibl-Eibesfeldt, *Love and Hate* 55.
45. Diem, *Weltgeschichte des Sports* 357.
46. Stephen G. Miller, "The Date of Olympic Festivals," *Mitteilungen des Deutschen Archäologischen Instituts: Athenische Abteilung* 90 (1975) 215–31.

the area of human activity in which we must search for the nature of sport. So far we have shown that, if we understand that sport is a form of ritual, we are capable of explaining the persistence of individual sports that appear, on the surface, to have outlived their original purpose. Indeed, we have shown that this feature is precisely what is characteristic of ritual. We have also divorced ritual from religion and shown that sport is not an outgrowth of religion. (If sport is frequently associated with religious practice, that is not surprising, for many ritual acts have at one time or another been associated with religion; but the connection between sport and religion, like that between ritual in general and religion, is not an essential one.) Thus there is no inconsistency in the flourishing of sports in societies that are "secularized." For ritual cannot be purged as readily as can religion. Indeed ritual flourishes as much in socialist countries as anywhere else. One could not find a more striking example of ritual than the effusive display of martial might that takes place in socialist countries every year on the first of May, the day traditionally associated with vegetation rituals. And, to take an example from the world of sport, when the "Friendship Games" were held for those socialist countries that refused to participate in the 1984 Olympic Games, the Soviet authorities could not dispense with the ritual that had become associated with international competition since 1896, namely the ceremonial lighting of a symbolic torch. But, since the "genuine" Olympic flame was elsewhere, the great bowl that had been built for the 1980 Olympic Games in Moscow was lit from the eternal flame that burns in the Kremlin in memory of the dead of World War II.[47] It should be noted that funeral games held in honor of warriors killed in battle are among the oldest rituals for which there is evidence.

The recognition that sport is a form of ritual behavior is not sufficient in and of itself for the understanding of the nature of sport. There are numerous human rituals that serve various functions and that have diverse origins. And if ritualized behavior is, as Lorenz puts it, behavior that "acquires an entirely new function, that of communication," we must still try to determine what the original function of sport was and what new function it has acquired—that is to say, what sport is "communicating." Now, I earlier indicated that a successful definition of sport ought to be able to account for the persistence of individual sports (which the definition of sport as ritual activity makes possible), but it ought also to explain the origin of sport and account for the great

---

47. *New York Times*, 19 August 1984, sec. 5, p. 7.

diversity of activities that comprise sport. This seems to be an unreasonable demand, since it involves the search for a single, unifying concept to account for the origin of sport, on the one hand, and the discovery of a principle, on the other, whereby we can explain how activities as varied as waterskiing, bullfighting and chariot racing can have arisen from a common source. But this is exactly what a definition ought to be expected to do, and the fact that no satisfactory theory of sport has yet been advanced is not an indication of the impossibility of the task. I should like to suggest a definition of sport, based upon our understanding that sport is to be sought among human ritual activities, that will account—if not completely, at least more fully than has been possible heretofore—for the origin of sport, and that will suggest why sport takes so many different forms. And that definition is as follows: Sport is the ritual sacrifice of physical energy.

Now that we have defined *ritual*, it remains only to define the term *sacrifice* for our definition to be intelligible. I must admit, however, that I am in no better position to define this notoriously problematic concept than anyone else. Still, a great deal of very important work has been done in recent years that has enabled us to come to a greater understanding of the nature of sacrificial ritual, and the perhaps questionable practice of defining one problematic concept in terms of another may have the compensatory advantage of shedding some light on both terms. For, just as researchers into the nature of sport have been content to ignore the importance of ritual in general and of sacrificial ritual in particular, so scholars concerned with the nature of sacrifice have neglected some of the evidence available to them by not considering the possibility that sport is an activity that ought to be of concern to them. If it is correct to regard sport as a form of ritual sacrifice, and if it is legitimate to speak of the "sacrifice" of something as apparently immaterial as "energy," then it would seem that some new avenues of approach to the notion of sacrifice are available.

To begin with, it is important to recognize that sacrifice is not necessarily, or originally, an offering of a gift to a deity. There is no evidence that belief in deities that are likely to be regarded as enjoying gifts is anterior in human development to the practice of sacrifice. And, in any case, it is difficult to see in what sense deities can be said to "enjoy" such gifts as, for example, the charred carcass of a lamb or locks of human hair.[48] Clearly the explanations given by sacrificers for their behavior are in many instances rationalizations. Human sacrifice at the

48. Jensen, *Myth and Cult* 165.

tomb of a deceased leader is "explained" by the need that the leader feels for servants or retainers in the afterlife. The practice of pouring libations is "explained" on the grounds that the deities under the earth, or the souls of the dead, are in need of drink. But these explanations are themselves inadequate and sometimes call for further explanation. The Greeks poured upon the ground libations to gods who were supposed to be in heaven, and the libations sometimes consisted of liquids that are not normally drunk, like olive oil.[49] The Hesiodic myth of Prometheus was devised to account for the fact that men burnt thighbones rather than (what would be equally difficult to account for) meat as a sacrifice to the gods.[50] Indeed, it is not an unreasonable hypothesis that the gods and belief in an afterlife are themselves part of this rationalization: once sacrifice began to be felt as in some sense a "gift," it became necessary to posit the existence of entities as beneficiaries of these gifts. This may sound like an instance of the cart before the horse: how can there be gifts without beneficiaries? In other words, is it not more reasonable to assume that the gods and the spirits of the dead existed before, and provided the impetus for, the transformation of abandonment into giving? In fact, it is more economical to suppose that the two developed pari passu. For the rationalization of sacrifice as a gift and the invention of the gods and the spirits of the dead both serve the same purpose—namely, to "explain" why sacrifice works.

Then why does sacrifice work? And what is sacrifice if it is not an offering of a gift to a deity? It would be presumptuous in the extreme to imagine that we can answer either of these questions with any kind of precision, or in a manner likely to secure general agreement. The best I can hope to do here is to make some tentative suggestions in the hope that those who are better equipped to do so will be able to advance the inquiry to a new level. We shall perhaps do best to follow in the footsteps of the great Swiss scholar Karl Meuli, who more than anyone else put the study of sacrifice on a firm basis by insisting upon proceeding from observed facts rather than from any presuppositions regarding beliefs or motivation. (I must also acknowledge a debt of gratitude to the work of Walter Burkert, who was the first to point out that Meuli's method and, in many instances, conclusions are compatible with those of the science of ethology.) What Meuli has shown, in his classic study

49. Burkert, *Structure* 41–42, 52; Meuli, "Griechische Opferbräuche" 192–93 (= *Gesammelte Schriften* II 915).
50. Meuli, "Griechische Opferbräuche" 213–15 (= *Gesammelte Schriften* II 937–38).

"Griechische Opferbräuche," is that the various forms of sacrifice do not derive from the same source. Rather, different forms of sacrifice can be traced back to different activities, some of which can be shown to go as far back in human history as the Stone Age. Indeed, by using material supplied by comparative ethology, Burkert shows that some of these activities are shared with other species, and are therefore likely to be even older than the development of mankind.

Meuli's study is divided into three parts, of unequal length, in each of which one form of sacrifice practiced by the ancient Greeks is examined. In the first part, Meuli shows that the practice—not, of course, confined to the ancient Greeks—of providing "meals" for the gods has its origin in customs that are widely observed among various peoples in connection with the treatment of the dead. In various societies death is, as it were, denied, and the dead are treated precisely as though they were still alive. In some instances the deceased is maintained in the home for a period of time, in some taken along on journeys, in some represented by a doll or other image. Some of these practices are not unknown today, such as embalming, the holding of wakes, and keeping photographs of the dead (which are sometimes addressed as though they were the persons themselves) about the house. But in most instances food is provided for the dead, and this practice survived in the Greek custom of laying out foodstuffs for the dead, for "heroes" and, occasionally, for the gods. Indeed, offerings of food for the dead are still made in parts of Greece today. The second part of Meuli's study concerns offerings that are consumed by fire or destroyed in some other manner. Among the ancient Greeks, as among many other peoples, these were conceived of as "gifts" to the dead. But Meuli shows conclusively that this was a later rationalization, and that the practice originated in the spontaneous destructive urge that accompanies, or is part of, the feeling of grief. Evidence for this urge comes in the form of widespread customs of mourning involving self-mutilation, killing of livestock or humans, and the destruction of various forms of property.

By far the longest, and surely the most brilliant and fascinating, part of Meuli's study is the third and last, in which the usual type of sacrifice made to the Olympian gods is examined. It was to explain this type of sacrifice that the myth of Prometheus was invented. In this ritual, the sacrificial animal was slaughtered near the altar of the god and the participants in the rite feasted upon the meat of the victim. The most curious part of the ritual, however, was the treatment of the inedible parts of the victim. The bones, the fat and, occasionally, portions from other parts of the victim's body were carefully placed together on the altar and burned. And, at the Athenian festival known as the Bouphonia, which in the fifth century B.C. was already considered to be a particularly old-fashioned ceremony,[51] after the feast the hide of the sacrificial ox was stuffed with hay, sewn up, and the animal, as though still alive, was yoked to a plough.[52] With the aid of copious and incontrovertible evidence, Meuli shows that this ritual derived from the practice of prehistoric hunters. The similarities, even down to the minutest details, between the classical Greek ritual and the practices of primitive hunters are so striking that it is impossible to disagree with Meuli's conclusion that the Olympian sacrifice of the Greeks was, in fact, ritual slaughter and feast. The practice of Mesolithic (and perhaps even Palaeolithic) hunters, observable among their modern descendants, was taken over by Asiatic herdsmen and subsequently by the Greeks of the historical period.

In origin, then, this form of sacrifice goes back to ritual behavior arising from the hunt. The primitive hunter purifies himself before the hunt by washing himself, by leaping over or running around a fire, and by putting on special clothes. Similarly, he who sacrifices must be pure, both among the Greeks and in other societies. Because the hunter feels a kinship with the beasts that he hunts, he considers it of great importance to kill his prey quickly and as painlessly as possible, and he often apologizes to the beast or assures the beast that the responsibility for its death lies elsewhere than with the hunter. Likewise the sacrificial animal must be slaughtered quickly and without resistance and the Athenians, in the abovementioned festival of the Bouphonia, went so far in the denial of responsibility for the slaughter that they put on trial for murder either the axe or the sacrificial knife that caused the death of the ox. Rather than simply disposing of those parts of the slain animal that are not consumed, the primitive hunter treats them with remarkable care. In fact, in many primitive societies the inedible parts are given funerals comparable to, or identical with, those given to men. The dead animal, that is, is treated as though it were still intact. The bones are arranged, or rearranged, in such a way as to suggest the intact skeleton of the beast. Often internal organs and bits from other parts of the animal's body are included in the arrangement. The skin is placed with this arrangement or is draped over a pile of rocks, a tree or a crude

51. Aristophanes, *Clouds* 984–85.
52. Porphyry, *On Abstinence* 2.30.2.

scaffolding specially prepared for this purpose. Greek sacrificial victims, and those of many other pastoral and agricultural societies, were ritually "reconstituted" in a similar manner.

What is the purpose of this curious and very widespread custom? Clearly the hunter is doing everything in his power to suggest, or even to bring about, the revivification of the animal that he has just slain. This is confirmed by the explicit statements of contemporary tribal hunters, who explain that they act as they do in order that their prey can be reborn. And this notion of resurrection is implicit in the Greek ritual of the Bouphonia and in many other rituals that are manifest survivals of this primitive hunting ceremony. In the case of these derivative, sacrificial rites, we are clearly dealing with a ritual in the sense of the word as defined above: the externals, at least, of the rite can be explained in terms of its origin; the treatment of the domestic, sacrificial animal is accounted for as a survival of the treatment of the wild prey by the primitive hunter. But what is the hunter's motivation? Meuli speaks of the hunter's "guilt" and "compassion," and certainly much of the hunter's behavior is well explained as arising from these emotions.[53] Burkert prefers to speak in terms of "anxiety."[54] It is difficult enough to apply these psychological terms to our own acquaintances; it is positively dangerous to attempt to impute motives to people who lived over fifteen thousand years ago and whose language we cannot know. For all we know, their motives may have been purely pragmatic: by revivifying their prey they may simply have hoped that the animal would live to fill their bellies again another day. So it is perhaps safest merely to assert that there is ample evidence that Palaeolithic hunters engaged in elaborate practices that appear to have been designed to undo the violence that their method of securing food entailed. And it is perhaps worth while to point out that behavior apparently designed to undo violence is not unknown elsewhere in the animal kingdom, where the application of psychological terms is even more questionable. Konrad Lorenz, for example, reports that Bernhard Grzimek told him "that an adult male chimpanzee, after having bitten him rather badly, seemed very concerned, after his rage had abated, about what he had done and tried to press together, with his fingers, the lips of Grzimek's worst

53. Meuli, "Griechische Opferbräuche" 228, 250–51 (= *Gesammelte Schriften* II 952, 978–79).

54. Burkert, *Homo Necans* 16; *Structure* 55; "Glaube und Verhalten: Zeichengehalt und Wirkungsmacht von Opferritualen," *Entretiens sur l'antiquité classique* 27 (1980) 91–125.

wounds."[55] It is as difficult to impute emotions like "guilt" and "anxiety" to Grzimek's assailant as it is to the nameless Stone Age hunters whose practices were the origin of blood sacrifice.

But the importance of Meuli's study lies in the fact that it shows, beyond the possibility of contradiction, how the practices of primitive hunters were ritualized and became the basis of one form of sacrifice. As Burkert puts it, "the original, pragmatic action [of] hunting and killing for food" was redirected:

> Hunting lost its basic function with the emergence of agriculture some ten thousand years ago. But hunting ritual had become so important that it could not be given up. Stability stayed with those groups who managed to make use of the social and psychological appeal of the ritual tradition by transforming, by redirecting, it until the whole action became a ritual. As the pragmatic importance declined, the symbolic value increased.[56]

What exactly that symbolic value was may perhaps be matter for debate. According to Burkert, what the ritual "communicates" is the arousal and appeasement of anxiety about bloodshed. This form of sacrifice persisted because "it established cooperation and solidarity by some kind of shared guilt, by traumatic repetition of bloodshed and killing; it tells and visibly demonstrates that Life is unique, but not autonomous; it must accept death in order to perpetuate itself."[57] What is of importance for our purposes is not whether Burkert's analysis is correct or not, but that *some* communicative purpose was served by the persistence and ritualization of the practices of Palaeolithic hunters.

We do not have the evidence that would enable us to tell whether Palaeolithic hunters themselves engaged in what we would consider "sport," but it cannot be denied that their actions became the basis of at least some forms of sport in pastoral and agricultural societies. For hunting and fishing are among the oldest and most widespread of sports. Why do men who do not depend upon these activities for their livelihood engage in hunting and fishing? The usual answer is something like, "Because they enjoy the challenge." But this is plainly inadequate as an explanation. To begin with, there are plenty of other potentially challenging activities, some of which can be pursued in the

55. Lorenz, *On Aggression* 249.
56. Burkert, *Structure* 54–55.
57. Ibid. 56.

healthful out-of-doors, that have not attracted numerous adherents. One might, for example, try climbing a tree with a goose strapped to one's chest, or reading Flaubert while hopping up and down in a canoe. In the second place, the "challenge" involved in hunting or fishing for sport has to be artificially enhanced; it is not the challenge inherent in the activity that accounts for its popularity. It is not "sporting" to net a trout or to shoot a sitting duck. One must do what the primitive hunter would never do, namely make the activity more difficult for oneself. Finally, the notion that the hunter hunts for sport because he enjoys the challenge explains only part of the activity that the hunter engages in. If, on the other hand, we recognize that hunting and fishing for sport are the ritualized descendants of activities that primitive hunters engaged in for purposes of survival, we can explain for the first time, for example, the practice of taxidermy. For, when the modern sportsman takes his marlin or his moose's head to be stuffed and mounted, he is doing nothing other than what his Palaeolithic ancestor did thirty thousand years ago.

Again, we are dealing with what is plainly a ritual activity, a pattern of behavior that has acquired a new, communicative function. The primitive hunter, after killing and eating his prey, sought by ritual means to revivify the slain animal. That basic and widespread pattern of behavior has two direct descendants in cultures that are not primarily hunting societies, namely blood sacrifice of domestic animals and the practice of hunting wild animals for sport. What communicative purpose is served by the former is a matter of debate. It is fairly clear what is communicated by the custom of killing wild animals and then displaying their seemingly revivified bodies. These stuffed animals or mounted heads have become "trophies," a word that has its origin in the military sphere and means literally "monuments of the rout of the enemy."[58] Such trophies of the hunt are intended to display the skill, the cunning, the bravery of the hunter, his power over the forces of nature. It is possible to trace a direct line of descent from the practices of the Palaeolithic hunters, who set up the skulls of their prey on stakes or in trees or who arranged the remains on specially built platforms, to the practices of more recent times.[59] Tribal hunters of recent times give,

58. For the ancient trophy, see A. B. Cook, *Zeus: A Study in Ancient Religion* II.1 (Cambridge, 1925) 108–13; A. J. Janssen, *Het antieke tropaion*, Verhandelingen van de Koninklijke Vlaamse Academie voor Wetenschappen, Klasse der Letteren 27 (Brussels, 1957).
59. Meuli, *Gesammelte Schriften* II 1083–1118.

or give back, the hide or the bones or the skull to the nature god or goddess, or to the "Master of Animals."[60] Greek and Roman hunters "dedicated" skull or hide or foot to some god or goddess both as a thank-offering for a successful hunt and as a bribe of sorts, in hopes that the deity would be kindly disposed in future.[61] By virtue of their effectiveness as means of influencing the will of the divine powers, these parts of the animal's body acquire a kind of magical potency. Hence the alleged aphrodisiac quality of the horn of the unfortunate white rhinoceros. Hence also the rabbit's foot that serves as a good-luck charm. Also as a good-luck charm antlers or horseshoes are hung, even today, in the gable or over the door of the house.

From customs like these comes the practice of using parts of the body for purposes of display and communication. In fox-hunting the mask, brush and pads (respectively the head, tail and feet of the animal) are the prerogative of the master of the hunt, and he has the privilege of awarding any of these as trophies to those of the followers whom he deems worthy. But, unlike his prehistoric forebear, the fox-hunter is not at all interested in the resurrection of his prey; the body is disdainfully thrown to the hounds. Similarly, the ears and the tail of the bull serve as marks of esteem for the exceptional matador. Neither is he interested in the flesh of his victim; the meat goes not to the killer but is sold or (in Mexico) patronizingly distributed to the poor.[62] The original purpose of the activity, namely to provide food for one's own sustenance, has been lost sight of, but the activity itself, even down to the special treatment of parts of the animal's body, has been preserved and persists for entirely different reasons, namely, for the purpose of display. And that aspect of the sport of hunting has been perfected with the development of the art of taxidermy. What the primitive hunter tried to do in a crude and rudimentary fashion, the modern technician can accomplish with such skill that it is impossible to tell at first glance whether the specimen is alive or dead. And this is an indication, not only of the skill of the taxidermist, but of that of the hunter as well. For, in addition to displaying the size and beauty of his prey, he is also demonstrating his ability to kill cleanly and quickly. This, too, is a feature of the primitive hunt, but the motivation is clearly different. The Lapp hunter who

60. Meuli, "Griechische Opferbräuche" 258–59 (= *Gesammelte Schriften* II 986–87).
61. Meuli, "Griechische Opferbräuche" 263 n. 5 (= *Gesammelte Schriften* II 991 n. 6).
62. For possible ritual origins of these practices, see Burkert, *Homo Necans* 38.

merely wounds a bear apologizes to the beast, presumably because of his compassion for the animal and because of his feelings of guilt at having caused its suffering.[63] Similarly, the domestic animal that is sacrificed must be dispatched quickly and with a single blow, for that is what is pleasing to the god in whose honor the beast is sacrificed.[64] The matador and the sportsman will protest and claim that they, too, are intent upon a clean and rapid kill because of their sympathy for the animal, and both will point to the etiquette of their sport, which prescribes that a wounded animal must be quickly put out of its misery. But that argument will not hold up under scrutiny. For, when the matador and the hunter assert that they wish to avoid any unnecessary suffering on the part of the animal, they are implying that some of the suffering is necessary. This can be the case, however, only for those who, like the primitive hunter, must kill in order to survive. I cannot deny that some, perhaps even most, hunters feel compassion toward their prey, but the primary reason for a quick and painless kill in hunting for sport is that it displays the skill of the hunter. We get confirmation of sorts from the practice of the fisherman. Since the angler's skill is displayed by hooking the fish and is independent of the degree of suffering that is imposed, he is not particularly concerned that the fish die quickly. He does not put it out of its misery, but allows it to suffocate slowly and quietly. Indeed, if the fish is to be mounted, suffocation is the preferred means of killing.

The angler, too, will protest at this point. The true sportsman, he will claim, is not concerned to kill fish at all; rather he throws them back as quickly as he catches them. We have heard this protest before and have dealt with its deficiency of logic above. But it is worth while to consider the sports fisherman briefly here. As we have seen, the practice of hunting and fishing for sport has evolved out of the practices of Palaeolithic men who, after killing and eating their prey, sought to revivify it. We have also seen that subsequent hunters maintained the practice of giving special treatment to the inedible parts of the animal, and that their reason in so doing was now to demonstrate their prowess and superiority over their prey. The fairly recent art of taxidermy serves to facilitate this demonstrative capacity. I am well aware that taxidermy serves as an adjunct, not only to sport, but to science as well; that it

63. Meuli, "Griechische Opferbräuche" 227 (= *Gesammelte Schriften* II 951–52).
64. Meuli, "Griechische Opferbräuche" 255, 268 (= *Gesammelte Schriften* II 983, 996–97).

helps in the study and classification of animals; that it has been avidly engaged in for the purposes of advancing human knowledge by such men as Charles Darwin, Prince Maximilian of Neuwied and the great American Sanskrit scholar William Dwight Whitney.[65] But science, too, in its own humane way, seeks to exercise dominion, by reducing to order, by systematizing, by formulating "laws." At any rate, the products of taxidermy serve to demonstrate with great eloquence the superiority of men over beasts. They assert, in effect, that man is capable of taking an animal's life and then preserving the body in a way that nature itself cannot do, immune from deterioration and in a pose of apparently sentient animation. In fact, it is the aim of the taxidermist to capture realistically the facial expression of his subject and to portray emotions. According to one manual,

> the large *Felidae* (tiger, lion, leopard, etc.) are the finest subjects for the taxidermist that the whole animal kingdom can produce. They offer the finest opportunities for . . . the expression of the various higher passions. . . . It frequently happens that the attitude desired for a feline or other carnivorous animal is one expressive of anger, rage, or defiance. For a single specimen, the most striking attitude possible is that of a beast at bay.[66]

In other words, what the taxidermist's customer specifically seeks is precisely what the primitive hunter wished to avoid. While the latter went to great lengths to allay the anger of the beast, the former attempts by artificial means to arouse it—the same purpose is served in the corrida by the picadores and the banderilleros, and in the rodeo by the bucking strap—in order to enhance the glory that attaches to the sportsman. And, while the primitive hunter often removes and disposes of the eyes of his prey so that the animal cannot see who his killer was,[67] the glass eye that the taxidermist inserts confronts the viewer with a lifelike and unflinching glare. But, no matter how successful the hunter and the taxidermist are in restoring the animal to life and in displaying man's power of life and death, the sports fisherman goes them one better. By luring the tasty trout into his power and then returning him to his haunts, the fisherman is, in effect, saying to the fish and for the benefit of all other witnesses, "I have it in my power to kill you and eat you.

65. For the latter, see C. Diehl, *Americans and German Scholarship: 1770–1870* (New Haven, Conn., 1978) 120.

66. W. T. Hornaday, *Taxidermy and Zoological Collecting* (New York, 1891) 171.

67. Meuli, "Griechische Opferbräuche" 243 (= *Gesammelte Schriften* II 970–71).

But I shall restore you to life." He has done, in fact, what the primitive hunter had only hoped to do.

But herein lies the difference between the primitive hunter and the sportsman. The former must kill, for he must eat. The latter is no longer dependent upon the hunt for his nourishment; his strength is maintained by consuming the produce of agriculture and the meat of domestic animals. Why, then, does man hunt and fish when he no longer needs to do so? Man hunted out of necessity for over 95 percent of his history. The patterns of behavior that developed over a period of more than one hundred thousand years have tended to persist precisely because those were the patterns of behavior that enabled man to develop successfully. Those patterns could not be eradicated in the relatively brief span of time since man has ceased depending upon hunting. Or, rather, there was no need for them to be abandoned, for they could be turned to a different purpose. Already in the Palaeolithic period the basic act of hunting had acquired certain ritual accessories. We do not know how long these ritual practices were in effect, but clearly they are of very long standing, for they became an indispensable feature of the hunt. And the entire complex of behavior, including what was originally a pragmatic action and what was originally a ritual activity, persisted and was redirected.

> For a living being lacking insight into the relation between causes and effects it must be extremely useful to cling to a behavior pattern which has once or many times proved to achieve its aim, and to have done so without danger. If one does not know which details of the whole performance are essential for its success as well as for its safety, it is best to cling to them all with slavish exactitude. . . . Even when a human being is aware of the purely fortuitous origin of a certain habit and knows that breaking it does not portend danger, nevertheless an undeniable anxiety impels him to observe it, and gradually the ingrained behavior becomes a custom.[68]

And so, even in a period of dependence upon agriculture and domesticated animals, the ancient Greeks and many other peoples engaged in ritual sacrifices that included all the elements of the rituals that the hunters had developed. And, just as these rituals had (apparently) been successful in securing for the hunter a continuation of his supply of

68. Lorenz, *On Aggression* 72.

food, so the ritual sacrifices were (apparently) successful in ensuring the goodwill of the gods toward the sacrificers.

But ritual sacrifice was not the only descendant of the practices of the primitive hunters. Pastoral and agricultural peoples continued to hunt "for sport," and also continued the ritual practices that had become ingrained behavior among those who had hunted of necessity. These practices included the ritual reconstitution of the victim. We have seen that taxidermy is a direct descendant of this practice. But there are other descendants as well. One of the practices employed by primitive hunters for the purpose of revivifying a slain animal is to dress up in the hide of the animal and to do a ritual dance.[69] This activity has itself suffered further ritualization and has persisted in various aspects even of contemporary society. *Swan Lake* and *The Firebird* are among the most conspicuous modern descendants. But another descendant is of perhaps greater relevance to our inquiry into the nature of sport. (Although, if our definition of sport as the ritual sacrifice of physical energy is correct, we may be justified in regarding ballet as a form of sport; after all, various forms of dancing are now represented at the Olympic Games and are engaged in as competitive sports.) For it is not only in the dance that animals are impersonated and animated. In America, for example, as an accompaniment to a ritual feast on Thanksgiving Day, it is customary to witness a football game played between teams with names like Bears, Rams and Lions. In many instances the players on these teams wear, as their uniforms, stylized representations of these totemic animals. It is characteristic of the ritual nature of this practice that the participants themselves are wholly unaware that the rite in which they are engaged goes back to the Stone Age.

We are able to trace the line of descent from the Palaeolithic hunters to the sportsmen of the present day with some confidence. It is reasonable to suppose that the origin of this practice was, as we have indicated, the desire to reanimate and revivify the slain animal by moving around vigorously while wearing the animal's skin. For that skin came from the animal, be it bear or buffalo, that provided the hunter with his means of livelihood. Wearing the hide of his prey also served to reinforce the sense of kinship that the hunter felt with the rest of the animal kingdom. But that sense of kinship is considerably attenuated when man ceases to depend upon hunting for food—that is to say, when he begins to hunt

---

69. Meuli, "Griechische Opferbräuche" 242 n. 2 (= *Gesammelte Schriften* II 969 n. 4).

"for sport." With the domestication of cattle, sheep and swine, and with the cultivation of crops, many animals previously hunted for food became "the enemy," since they prey on domesticated flocks and diminish the produce of the fields. But the ritual existed, and it persisted because it could be successfully redirected. In addition to dressing in an animal's hide in order to bring the dead to life and thereby to ensure a continuing supply of food, man began to impersonate other species for a new purpose, namely to assume the attributes of those species. Burkert calls attention to a wall painting from Neolithic Turkey showing men dressed in leopard skins hunting stag and boar. He is likely right to interpret the activity as a ritual hunt and the men as "a group of priests or initiates who imitate predators."[70] This must be a new practice, since it represents a transference from the original one: instead of dressing in the hide of the *sacrificial* animal, the sacrificer assumes the attributes of the beast of prey, perhaps in order to transfer the guilt for the slaughter from men to the "natural" enemy of the sacrificial beast. At any rate, the original practice of donning the hide of the hunted animal persisted long after the end of the Neolithic period, in the form of sacrificial rituals in which the hide of the sacrificial animal was worn by the priest or by those on whose behalf the sacrifice was performed.[71] But it is not only hunters and those who preside over blood sacrifice who seek to assume the attributes of animals. It is not uncommon for participants in various sports in many societies, including our own, to appropriate some of the physical characteristics of animals so as to share in the speed, strength or courage of those animals.

For example, it is reported of the Dakota Indians of Minnesota, when they play a game similar to lacrosse, that "the players frequently hang to the belt the tail of a deer, antelope, or some other fleet animal, or the wings of swift-flying birds, with the idea that through these they are endowed with the swiftness of the animal."[72] In the ball games of the Choctaw Indians of Oklahoma, "it is a rule of the play that no man shall wear moccasins on his feet, or any other dress than his breechcloth around his waist, with . . . a 'tail' made of white horsehair or quills, and a 'mane' on the neck, of horsehair dyed of various colors."[73] One type of Roman gladiator was called a *myrmillo,* his name deriving

70. Burkert, *Structure* 55.
71. See, e.g., Burkert, *Homo Necans* 115; Gaster, *Myth, Legend, and Custom in the Old Testament* 165–82; Hubert and Mauss, *Sacrifice* 39.
72. Culin, *Games of the North American Indians* 612.
73. Ibid. 600.

from a fish that adorned his helmet. (This was not a real fish but the representation of one. We are now on familiar ground, for there is an American football team that has representations of dolphins on its helmets. But there is no essential difference between the practice of modern football players and that of primitive sportsmen, who used parts of the animals themselves rather than symbolic images of them.) Another example is provided by the Cherokee Indians of North Carolina, who wear in their ball games nothing other than a pair of shorts and an ornament in their hair. The latter "is made up of an eagle's feathers, to give keenness of sight; a deer tail, to give swiftness; and a snake's rattle, to render the wearer terrible to his adversaries. If an eagle's feathers can not be procured, those of a hawk or any other swift bird of prey are used."[74] It should be clear, then, that the practice of ritually assuming the properties of various animals in connection with sports events is very widespread and derives directly from the practice of the primitive hunt.

It will be worth while at this point to examine in some detail a ball game of the abovementioned Cherokee Indians, since it will become clear from this examination how many other elements of this game and the rituals surrounding it are descendants of primitive hunting practices. I have chosen the Cherokee ball game because there is a very full ethnographic account of it available, written with remarkably few preconceptions and with many valuable details such as are often omitted from descriptions of sports and games.[75] For historians of sport tend to be interested exclusively in the details of the game itself, and frequently omit descriptions of the rituals (which, for the participants, are often no less important than the actual contest) that are connected with it; and anthropologists are sometimes lacking in interest in sports. Also, there is no reason to believe that this particular game, which is a form of lacrosse, is in any sense a direct descendant of hunting, so that a special effort will be necessary in order to explain the numerous elements that the primitive hunt and the ritual surrounding this game have in common.

To begin with, this ball game is only played during a certain time of the year, from midsummer until the onset of cold weather in winter. In his account, James Mooney gives a partial explanation, saying that, since

74. Mooney, "Cherokee Ball-Play" 122 (= Culin, *Games of the North American Indians* 581).
75. Mooney, "Cherokee Ball-Play," quoted at length by Culin (*Games of the North American Indians* 575–86).

the players are only lightly clad, they cannot prolong the playing season into winter. But that does not explain why the players do not play in winter wearing warm clothing, or why they do not play at all in the spring or early summer. Rather this game, like many sports in various societies, including our own, represents the adaptation of hunting ritual to an agricultural society. Specific sports are played at specific times of the year because, as ritual sacrifices, they are intended to have a particular effect upon the weather or upon the crops or upon the fecundity of the flocks. Another feature of the Cherokee game that has clear associations both with ritual sacrifice and with primitive hunting ritual is the fact that the players are subject to certain very strict taboos. During the period of training for the game, the participant must refrain from eating rabbit or frog, both of which are regular items in the Cherokee diet.[76] This taboo is explained on the grounds that the former is a timid animal and the bones of the latter are brittle, but this is clearly a secondary rationalization. These ball players are subject to the same kind of taboo that the hunter is subject to before the hunt. The Indians of Nootka Sound on Vancouver Island fast for a week before they go out to catch whales; the Baganda fishermen of Uganda eat no meat while they are fishing; while they are engaged in trapping eagles, the Hidatsa Indians of North Dakota fast during the daytime; the headman in charge of the fishing for turtle in the village of Bulaa, New Guinea, eats only bananas while the nets are being made.[77]

Other foods are avoided by the Cherokee ball players while they are in training, including a certain kind of fish and a particular herb, as well as "hot food and salt."[78] The prohibition against salt is also paralleled among tribal hunters and fishers: the abovementioned Baganda fishermen may not eat salt, nor may the hunters of the Indonesian island of Nias during the period in which they are preparing pitfalls as animal traps.[79] What is the significance of these taboos? Clearly by refraining from salt and from cooked food, the conspicuous indicators of human diet, the Cherokee is somehow denying his human status and declaring his assimilation to the animal. But to what end? He is not a hunter but a ball player. I would suggest with some confidence that he is, in fact, a

---

76. Mooney, "Cherokee Ball-Play" 110 (= Culin, *Games of the North American Indians* 575).

77. Frazer, *Taboo* 191 (Nootka Sound), 194 (Uganda), 199 (Hidatsa), 192 (Bulaa).

78. Mooney, "Cherokee Ball-Play" 110 (= Culin, *Games of the North American Indians* 575).

79. Frazer, *Taboo* 194, 196.

sacrificial animal. We shall see even more clearly in the following essay, when we examine sports among the ancient Greeks, that the athlete is in a sense a substitute for the sacrificial animal, but it is helpful to have this Amerindian evidence as confirmation. Indeed, there are numerous and striking parallels between the practice of the Greeks in connection with athletics and that of the Indian ball players and, since there is of course no question of direct contact, we must assume that these ball games and the Olympic Games have a common origin. Further, since we are able to find significant associations between primitive hunting ritual on the one hand and the details of Cherokee and, as we shall see, Greek sports on the other, it is reasonable to assume that the common origin is to be sought among the practices of prehistoric hunters.

In addition to prohibitions against specific foods, the Cherokee taboo includes a prohibition against intercourse with women. According to Mooney, the period of taboo "always lasts for seven days preceding the game, but in most cases is enforced for twenty-eight days—*i.e.,* 4 × 7—four and seven being sacred numbers."[80] There is a more reasonable explanation, however, for the 28-day period than Mooney's numerology. The length of the period of taboo is determined not in connection with the prohibitions against food, as Mooney's arrangement of the material might suggest, but in connection with this latter prohibition against intercourse. Again, parallels are available from hunting societies. The magician who performs the ceremonies that ensure success in hunting the wallaby among the natives of New Guinea must refrain from intercourse with his wife for one month before the time of the hunt. The Carrier Indians of British Columbia refrain from intercourse for one month before they set their bear traps.[81] Surely the purpose of this prohibition is to prevent the hunter or the athlete from impregnating a woman, the result of which would be that his vital force would be diminished and, along with it, his likelihood of success. This is confirmed by the further provision among the Cherokee that, "should a player's wife be with child, he is not allowed to take part in the game under any circumstances, as he is then believed to be heavy and sluggish in his movements, having lost just so much of his strength as has gone to the child."[82] Taboos prohibiting intercourse with women are ex-

80. Mooney, "Cherokee Ball-Play" 110 (= Culin, *Games of the North American Indians* 575).
81. Frazer, *Taboo* 193, 197.
82. Mooney, "Cherokee Ball-Play" 111 (= Culin, *Games of the North American Indians* 576).

tremely common in various societies both before hunts and before warfare, although the period of taboo is usually reduced to a few days or
merely to the night before the hunt or battle. It is also, I am told, a
common superstition among athletes even today that intercourse reduces athletic achievement. And so some athletes refrain from intercourse before a sports event, just as their Palaeolithic forebears exercised
continence before hunting. American football coaches often impose
strict curfews on their players and enforce dietary regulations by sub-
jecting players to a ritual "training meal" immediately before a game.
This practice is alleged to be purely pragmatic: the player must be fed
the "right" foods for optimum performance and he must get enough
sleep so that his strength will not be diminished. But, as we have seen,
this type of practice has been known since long before the days of scientific training programs for athletes.

Again, there is a striking parallel to the Cherokee practice among the
ancient Greeks. For a period of one month before the beginning of the
Olympic Games, all participants in the games were required to live and
train in the city of Elis under the strict supervision of the Olympic
authorities. We do not know the details of this enforced training program (which, in any case, was no doubt modified considerably during
the thousand-year existence of the ancient games), but it is clear that it
was a rigorous program that had the effect of ensuring that only the
most highly qualified athletes participated in the actual games. Since the
participants in the Olympic Games came from all over the Greek world,
and since married women were prohibited from witnessing the games,
it is unlikely that a wife would have accompanied her husband during
this one-month period of training. The effect of this requirement, therefore, would have been the same as the Cherokee's taboo, and we may
be inclined to believe that the reason for it was likewise the same,
namely to prevent the athlete from engaging in sexual intercourse before the games. And, when we consider the fact that the athlete's diet
was strictly regulated by the Olympic authorities during this one-
month period, it becomes likelier still that this enforced period of training was of ritual origin and existed for the purpose of enforcing taboos.[83] Our sources do not tell us specifically what kind of diet the
authorities imposed upon the participants, and the diet too, like other
elements of the training program, was subject to change over the course
of many years. But we are told—and the comparative material adduced

---

83. Brelich, *Paides e parthenoi* 454.

above encourages us to believe the account—that in the earliest times Greek athletes did not include meat in their training diet.[84]

The prohibition against intercourse with women among the Cherokee ball players continues for a period of seven days following a game. This taboo also derives from the practice of primitive hunters, although it is not nearly so common as the prohibition of intercourse before the hunt. The wife of a Hottentot could not approach her husband for a period of three days after he had killed a large beast. And Lapp hunters may not sleep with their wives for three, or in some cases five, days after they have killed a bear.[85] The reason for this, apparently, is that the hunter and the athlete must be ritually pure during the hunt or during the game, and it is quite common for various kinds of purification ceremonies to be performed both before and after the hunt and the game. These ceremonies take the form either of ritual washing or of fumigation. The Cherokees, like many other peoples, use both forms. On the night before a game, a dance is held. From the time of this dance until after the game is over the next afternoon, the players eat nothing at all. "The dance must be held close to the river, to enable the players to 'go to water' during the night."[86] This ceremony, which the players engage in frequently during their period of training and again several times both during the dance and on the way from the scene of the dance to that of the game itself, is a particularly solemn rite of purification, which culminates in the ritual washing of the head and chest in the water of the river. Likewise the whalers of Nootka Sound wash themselves several times a day in preparation for their fishing expeditions. The headman of the village of Bulaa washes himself every evening at sundown while the fishermen make the nets to catch dugong. "Among the Tsetsaut Indians of British Columbia hunters who desire to secure good luck fast and wash their bodies with ginger-root for three or four days."[87] The victorious Cherokee ball players also "go to water" immediately after the contest, just as many tribal hunters wash themselves after, as well as before, the hunt.[88] Likewise it is customary for those

84. Pausanias, *Description of Greece* 6.7.10; Diogenes Laertius, *Lives of the Philosophers* 8.12.

85. Frazer, *Taboo* 220, 221.

86. Mooney, "Cherokee Ball-Play" 114 (= Culin, *Games of the North American Indians* 576).

87. Frazer, *Taboo* 191 (Nootka Sound), 192 (Bulaa), 198 (Tsetsaut).

88. Mooney, "Cherokee Ball-Play" 131 (= Culin, *Games of the North American Indians* 586); Meuli, "Griechische Opferbräuche" 226 (= *Gesammelte Schriften* II 951); Frazer, *Taboo* 207, 219–22.

sacrificing to wash before and after the ritual.[89] Similar ritual lustrations are also common among athletes in various societies. The ancient Greeks normally located their gymnasia near a river for the same reason that the Cherokees held their dance near a river. The site of the ancient Olympic Games is at the confluence of two rivers and, indeed, there is a remarkable similarity between the opening of the Olympic Games and the preparation for the Cherokee ball game. Just as the Cherokee ball players proceed from the site of the dance to the scene of the contest, making periodic stops along the way to "go to water," so the ancient Greeks held a procession of all the athletes and officials from the city of Elis to the site of Olympia. The procession followed a route known as the Sacred Way, and along this route was a fountain named Piera, at which the procession was required to stop for the purposes of a ceremony of purification.

The ancient Greeks regularly bathed after they engaged in athletic exercise, but there is also some evidence for bathing before exercise. There is, for example, a fifth-century vase painting showing Atalanta preparing for her wrestling match with Peleus by bathing and oiling her body.[90] Similarly, Nausicaa and her attendants bathed and oiled their bodies before eating and playing ball.[91] Similar purificatory rites are practiced by athletes of other societies in connection with sports events. Bathing after exercise is too common to require illustration. Before matches, sumo wrestlers purify themselves by rinsing out their mouths with water.[92] The ring in which the matches are held is also purified by sprinklings of water and salt. Swimmers in international competition now regularly take a hot shower, sometimes followed by a cold one, before a race. Now, it may be objected that this practice is based upon scientific principles[93] and therefore cannot be of ritual origin. But there is no inconsistency. Ritual practices persist because they are conducive to success. They are subject to the same kind of natural selection as organisms. Science can give a rational account of why a particular ritual is conducive to success, and therefore of why it has persisted. (It should

89. Meuli, "Griechische Opferbräuche" 253–54, 264–65 (= *Gesammelte Schriften* II 981–82, 993); Hubert and Mauss, *Sacrifice* 22.

90. Ginouvès, *Balaneutikè* 117–18, fig. 68.

91. *Odyssey* 6.96.

92. J. A. Sargeant, *Sumo: The Sport and the Tradition* (Rutland, Vt., 1959) 73. For rinsing out the mouth in preparation for sacrifice, see Hubert and Mauss, *Sacrifice* 21–22.

93. See F. Carlile, "Effect of Preliminary Passive Warming on Swimming Performance," *Research Quarterly* 27 (1956) 143–51.

be noted that in many instances myths serve the same purpose, namely, to account for the persistence of a particular ritual.[94]) The same can be said for the persistence of the ritual sport in general. The scientist may be able to tell us that sport is conducive to success because it promotes physical fitness (although not all sports do this), and the social scientist may be able to tell us that sport is conducive to success because it helps to delineate social relationships (although not all sports do this either). But people engage in sport today for the same reason they have always engaged in sport, namely because they have always engaged in sport.

Athletes wash themselves after exercise not because the odor of perspiration is unpleasant. The odor of perspiration is unpleasant (to some, but not to all) because it is associated with those who have not yet ritually purified themselves. To assert that we "civilized" folk wash ourselves for "aesthetic" reasons is to make the same mistake of motivation that we noticed earlier in connection with lipstick and pierced ears. And in any case this alleged aesthetic consideration can have nothing to do with the practice of ritual ablutions *before* exercise or competition. On more than one occasion I have witnessed an East German swimmer, a paragon of pragmatic materialism, kneel down beside the pool before a race for the purpose of scooping up some water with which to perform these ablutions. And it is not uncommon in swimming races to see an intentional false start, so that the competitors will get the "feel" of the water before the contest. These are not risible superstitions. They serve a legitimate purpose, namely to calm the nerves, to reduce anxiety. But this is precisely what is characteristic of ritual behavior: "Even when a human being is aware of the purely fortuitous origin of a certain habit and knows that breaking it does not portend danger, nevertheless an undeniable anxiety impels him to observe it."[95] And so the East German swimmer, like the Cherokee, washes before the contest.

But the Cherokee ball players purify themselves before the game not only with water but with fire. For the dance in which they participate during the whole of the night preceding the game takes place in a circle around the fire. "At the final dance green pine tops are thrown upon the fire, so as to produce a thick smoke, which envelopes the dancers."[96] The same kind of ritual purification is common among tribal hunters. On the night before they hunt deer, the Huichol Indians of Mexico

---

94. Burkert, *Structure* 57.
95. Lorenz, *On Aggression* 72.
96. Mooney, "Cherokee Ball-Play" 119 (= Culin, *Games of the North American Indians* 579).

gather around the fire.[97] And many of the hunters living within the Arctic Circle perform similar purificatory rites before the hunt, leaping over a fire or dancing around it or fumigating themselves with the smoke of branches or aromatic herbs that are thrown into the fire.[98] Likewise those who perform sacrifices are also frequently purified by means of fire or the smoke of fire.[99] This practice persists today in the use of incense in some forms of worship. And similarly athletes are occasionally subjected to this kind of ritual purification. Before a footrace Zuñi Indians of New Mexico engage in a ceremony in which a cigarette is passed around from one runner to another. The Choctaw Indians have a ritual similar to that of the Cherokees, in which the night before a lacrosse game is spent in dancing about a fire.[100] Similar bonfires are common on college campuses in the United States, and around them are held ceremonies that, the participants are convinced, are conducive to victory in the football game to be held the following day. The fire ceremony now connected with the opening of the Olympic Games is perhaps also to be ascribed to similar origins.

At the dance that the Cherokees hold on the evening before the game, the players are dressed as they will be during the game itself, that is, they are wearing nothing but a loincloth or a pair of shorts. It is characteristic of sports events that the participants change out of their everyday clothes for the purposes of the contest. Today, of course, this practice has developed to the point where the clothing worn for sport is determined by pragmatic considerations. Players on different sides wear uniforms of different colors in order to be more readily distinguishable. Costumes are designed in such a way as to prevent or minimize injuries or to enhance the athlete's performance. The cumbrous protective equipment worn by the goalie on an ice-hockey team is an example of the former; the sleek aerodynamic design of the speedskater's outfit exemplifies the latter. But all of this is a secondary development, for it has always been the custom of athletes to signify their participation in sport by wearing some costume different from that normally worn outside of the context of sport, even if, as is sometimes the case, their costume actually interferes with their performance or increases the danger to themselves. Ancient Greek wrestlers, for example,

97. Frazer, *Taboo* 197.
98. Meuli, "Griechische Opferbräuche" 226 (= *Gesammelte Schriften* II 950–51).
99. Meuli, "Griechische Opferbräuche" 254, 265 (= *Gesammelte Schriften* II 982, 993–94).
100. Culin, *Games of the North American Indians* 684 (Zuñi), 599–601 (Choctaw).

competed totally naked, exposing their genitals to public view and, one would think, to considerable risk. Even today, participants in judo and equitation wear costumes that are not designed entirely from the point of view of practicality. Their purpose is as much ceremonial as it is functional. The origin of this custom of wearing special clothing for sport lies in the practice of the primitive hunters, who change into different—that is to say, ritually pure—clothing in order to hunt.[101] From this practice also derives the custom of wearing special clothing during sacrifice.[102]

The sacrificial character of the Cherokee ritual will become clearer when we consider the next feature of it. When the ball players have arrived at the place where the game is to be played, they are subjected to a painful ordeal. Each player submits to having his flesh scored countless times with a sort of comb whose teeth are made of splinters of turkey bone. The arms, legs and body of the player are so treated that, by the end of the ordeal, "the blood is trickling in little streams from nearly three hundred gashes. None of the scratches are deep, but they are unquestionably very painful, as all agree who have undergone the operation."[103] One would think that this ordeal, combined with the effects of the preceding fasting and vigil, would render the player less qualified to perform adequately in the game. "Nevertheless the young men endure the ordeal willingly and almost cheerfully, regarding it as a necessary part of the ritual to secure success in the game."[104] How can we account for this curious and painful custom? Well, it is by no means an isolated phenomenon. The abovementioned whalers of Vancouver prepared for their hunt by fasting, by refraining from sexual intercourse, by bathing frequently, and by rubbing "their bodies, limbs, and faces with shells and bushes till they looked as if they had been severely torn with briars."[105] They made similar preparations before going out to war.[106] Such mutilations, and others of an even more severe nature, are used by members of other tribes in preparation for warfare. But by far the most frequent application of such ritual mutilations is in connec-

101. Meuli, "Griechische Opferbräuche" 226 (= Gesammelte Schriften II 951).

102. Hubert and Mauss, Sacrifice 22; Meuli, "Griechische Opferbräuche" 253–54, 264 (= Gesammelte Schriften II 981–82, 993).

103. Mooney, "Cherokee Ball-Play" 121–22 (= Culin, Games of the North American Indians 580).

104. Mooney, "Cherokee Ball-Play" 122 (= Culin, Games of the North American Indians 580).

105. Frazer, Taboo 191.

106. Ibid. 160–61.

tion with mourning for the dead. Scores of examples of this sort of behavior as a form of ritual lamentation are given by Frazer in his *Folk-Lore in the Old Testament* and by Gaster in his *Myth, Legend, and Custom in the Old Testament*.[107] We may safely discard the latter's interpretation that the mutilation exists for the purpose of drawing blood to quench the thirst of the dead, and that similarly the cutting of hair for the dead serves to provide a meal to satisfy the hunger of the deceased. But the frequency and the widespread occurrence of these practices in connection with mourning indicates that it is to this connection that we should look for an explanation. In fact, the appropriate explanation had already been given by Karl Meuli in his article "Griechische Opferbräuche," to which I have referred above.[108] The various ritual manifestations of mourning—tearing the hair, lacerating the body with one's nails, beating the breast, rending one's garments, destroying one's possessions and so forth—are all ritualized acts that derive from the spontaneous reaction to bereavement, a reaction that involves destructive, and self-destructive, impulses. (We can see what is perhaps the same impulse in action among young children who, when they are frustrated or are prevented from doing what they want, sometimes go into a fit of destructiveness, breaking their own toys, crying and even biting themselves.) The notion that the blood, the hair, the objects destroyed, are "gifts" to the dead is only a secondary development.

The particular form of the Cherokee mutilation—scoring the skin with an implement designed to produce parallel superficial gashes—gives every indication of being a ritualized form of lamentation, with the gashes resembling those left by mourners who rake their own bodies with their nails. And there is another feature of the ritual that encourages us to make this connection. It will be remembered that at the climax of the dance that precedes the game, the participants are fumigated by the smoke of pine branches that are thrown upon the fire. According to Mooney, this is the same ceremony that is performed "when there has recently been a death in the settlement."[109] But what is the connection between ritual lamentation and the lacrosse game that the Cherokees are about to play? And what is the connection between

---

107. J. G. Frazer, *Folk-Lore in the Old Testament* III (London, 1918) 270–303; Gaster, *Myth, Legend, and Custom in the Old Testament* 590–602.
108. Meuli, "Griechische Opferbräuche" 201–9 (= *Gesammelte Schriften* II 924–34). Cf. also *Gesammelte Schriften* I 333–85, II 887–88.
109. Mooney, "Cherokee Ball-Play" 120 (= Culin, *Games of the North American Indians* 579).

ritual lamentation and the rituals derived from the practice of primitive hunters? And, to complete the circle, what is the connection between these latter rituals and the game of the Cherokees? I should like to suggest that these are all forms of ritual sacrifice, and that they operate in parallel. There is no specific connection between the ritualized lamentation and the ball game. But they are both forms of ritual sacrifice, having very different origins, that the players engage in for the same purpose. They are alternatives, both of which are employed in order to make the likelihood of success even greater, although, in the course of development, one has become subordinated to the other, so that the Cherokees believe that ritual mutilation conduces to the success of the ritual ball game. Such multiplication of alternatives is not uncommon in ritual practice. In the Attic rite of the Bouphonia, for example, to which reference has been made above, two different kinds of sacrifice took place, but the ritual combined them in such a way as to impart an apparently causal relationship to them. The primary event of the ritual was the sacrifice to Zeus of an ox, a practice that, as Meuli has shown, derived from primitive hunting ritual.[110] But the setting out of a mixture of wheat and barley on the altar of Zeus was also part of the ritual. Meuli has reasonably traced the origin of this sort of practice to the custom of "feeding" the dead.[111] At any rate, both practices are clearly of different origins, and both were alternative forms of sacrifice aimed at the same purpose—namely, providing a meal for the god Zeus. But, in the course of the ceremony, the ox was led around the altar upon which the grain had been placed, and its inevitable attempt to eat the grain brought about its slaughter as a punishment for this impiety. These two forms of sacrifice were combined in order to increase the efficacy of the rite, but one form was subordinated to the other in order to provide a "motive" for it. Just so the mutilation and the Cherokee ball game are both forms of ritual sacrifice, but they have been combined in this ritual in such a way that the former is felt to increase the efficacy of the latter.

But in what sense are the mutilation and the ball game "sacrifices," and how did they come to be associated with the other elements that make up the ritual connected with the game? At this point it is best to

110. Meuli, "Griechische Opferbräuche" 211–87 (= *Gesammelte Schriften* II 935–1018). For the Bouphonia, see H. W. Parke, *Festivals of the Athenians* (London, 1977) 162–67.

111. Meuli, "Griechische Opferbräuche" 189–201 (= *Gesammelte Schriften* II 911–24).

recapitulate briefly what we have learned so far. Primitive hunters developed the practice of ritually "reconstituting" their prey after killing it. This custom of killing and revivifying persisted in societies even after they had ceased to be dependent upon hunting for their food. The custom persisted in two forms. On the one hand, the practice of blood sacrifice, in which a domestic animal is substituted for the wild beast, is a direct descendant of the practices of the Palaeolithic hunters. On the other hand, these primitive practices are also the ancestors of certain sports, such as hunting and fishing in the wild, the so-called "hunts" of the Roman amphitheater and the Spanish bullfight. We have also seen that a remarkable number of the practices associated with sport in general—taboos, purifications, uniforms—derive from the primitive hunting ritual. But we can only account for a limited number of specific sports (including, perhaps, the javelin throw and archery) as direct descendants of the primitive hunt.[112] There seems to be no possibility of accounting for golf or waterskiing or the Cherokee lacrosse game in this way. But by the same token, it is not possible to account for all forms of sacrifice as deriving from the practice of the primitive hunter. Sacrifice exists in a great variety of forms, including human sacrifice, libations, hair-offerings and so on. Meuli was very careful to keep the various forms separate and to insist that each form had its own origin. Indeed, it is difficult to see what the relationship is between blood sacrifice, on the one hand, and libations, for example, on the other. For in the one the meat is consumed by the sacrificer, while in the other the sacrificer pours the wine, milk or oil out upon the ground. Likewise it is difficult to see what the relationship is between fox-hunting on the one hand and badminton on the other.

But it is always a useful principle that two problems are better than one. And in this case in particular the two problems are so similar that it is reasonable to believe that they are related. Let us look once again at the survival of primitive hunting ritual in blood sacrifice. Meuli's demonstration that the latter derived from the former is so convincing, and the number of correspondences between the two is so great, that there is a tendency to overlook the one striking difference between them. Blood sacrifice retains and repeats all of the external features of the primitive hunt with one big exception, the actual hunting and capture of the animal. Conspicuously absent from the ritual of blood sacrifice is the expenditure of energy that is so prominent a feature of the

112. See, for example, D. Morris, *The Soccer Tribe* (London, 1981).

hunt itself. (To be sure, the domestic animal to be sacrificed is often treated as though it were wild,[113] but this is a mere fiction that is more convincingly enacted outside the context of sacrifice, namely in the bull-ring and the rodeo.) Another striking feature of blood sacrifice is the fact that, in contrast to other forms of sacrifice, nothing is actually "sacrificed," or given up. The victim provides a meal for the sacrificers, and it is only those parts of the animal that are of no further use that are "given" to the gods. This fact puzzled even the ancient Greeks themselves, among whom blood sacrifice was a common occurrence,[114] just as it has puzzled modern investigators. Obviously the "gift" of the fat and the bones to the gods is a secondary development. But why should there be a gift at all? Meuli explains that the ritual reconstitution of the animal is designed to "give back" to the animal that which it needs for its regeneration.[115] But this formulation is influenced by the later development of hunting ritual into blood sacrifice. There is no reason to speak in terms of "giving" to the animal—in any case, part of the function of the primitive hunting ritual is to deny forcibly that anything has been taken—except when we view the hunting ritual in the light of other forms of sacrifice. But the hunting ritual is not itself a form of sacrifice. Rather it is the direct ancestor of blood sacrifice. The question that needs answering is: Why has the descendant of the primitive hunting ritual become assimilated to the other forms of sacrifice, in which something is, in fact, given up?

The answer, I think, lies in the expenditure of energy that is a feature of the hunt. Blood sacrifice ritualizes a human activity that involves the using up of something for the purpose of gaining something. In the hunt man expends a great deal of energy in order to secure the food necessary for further expenditure of energy. It is in this respect that the primitive hunt resembles libations, for example, in which wealth in the form of liquids is squandered in the expectation that equal or greater wealth will be secured. When, with the domestication of animals, the hunt became blood sacrifice, the element that disappeared from the ritual was the conspicuous expenditure of energy, and the required notion of "giving up" was transferred to the practice of "giving up" parts of the animal. But it is characteristic of humans that patterns of behavior do not simply die out. The element that is absent from the blood sac-

113. Burkert, *Homo Necans* 15–16.
114. Ibid. 7.
115. Meuli, "Griechische Opferbräuche" 237 (= *Gesammelte Schriften* II 964).

rifice persisted and was itself ritualized. It became sport, which is itself a form of sacrifice. For only if sport is a form of sacrifice can we explain its ritual associations. There is no other plausible reason to account for the fact that the Hurons played a game of lacrosse in order to influence the weather for the benefit of their crops.[116] It is only because they are engaged in ritual sacrifice that natives of the Sudan hold wrestling matches at the time of sowing and harvesting.[117] In Homer's *Iliad* the hero Achilles honors the death of his companion Patroclus with an elaborate funeral that consists of various kinds of sacrifice: hair-offering, holocausts of sheep and cattle, libations of oil, honey and wine, slaughter of horses and dogs, human sacrifice and . . . athletic contests.[118]

The common denominator is expenditure, waste, squandering.[119] The ritual of the Stone Age hunter had ingrained in the mind of man, as Walter Burkert so eloquently demonstrates in *Homo Necans,* the message that man must kill in order to live, that life entails death. Burkert and, before him, Meuli concentrated on the act of killing, because they were concerned with the survival of primitive hunting practice in sacrificial ritual, and it is the act of killing that the ritual of blood sacrifice ceremonializes. But primitive hunting practice also survives in the sport of hunting, and the message encoded by this ritual is that one must give up something of oneself in order to live. It is not only that the life of the beast must be "taken" in order for the hunter to survive; the hunter must give of his own energy in order to get. Once this becomes the message that the ritual is intended to communicate, two things happen. In the first place, it no longer matters on what the energy is expended. Whether effort is squandered hunting a fox, throwing the caber or running twenty-six miles, the message is the same, just as the same message is communicated whether one immolates a yearling lamb, leaves fruit to rot upon the altar or gives alms to the poor. In the second place, as we have seen to be the case generally with ritual practice, there is a tendency for the communication to be enhanced by means of repetition and exaggeration. If it is necessary to give up in order to get, then, according to the logic of ritual, the more one gives up, the more one is likely to get. In the case of other forms of sacrifice, this results in the

116. See M. A. Salter, "Meteorological Play-Forms of the Eastern Woodlands," *History of Physical Education and Sport: Research and Studies* 3 (1975–76) 11–23, especially 12.

117. Diem, *Weltgeschichte des Sports* 84.

118. *Iliad* 23. 141–259.

119. Cf. R. Caillois, *Man, Play, and Games,* English translation (New York, 1961) 5–6: "Play is an occasion of pure waste: waste of time, energy, ingenuity, skill."

making of ever more elaborate and expensive offerings. The most extravagant example, perhaps, is the famous potlatch of the natives of the west coast of North America, in which the greatest amount of prestige is secured by him who is capable of removing from circulation the greatest amount of wealth. (This custom survives today on an international scale in the arms race, the object of which is to impoverish other nations by forcing them to compete in squandering vast sums of money on costly weapons systems that will never be used.) This practice serves to communicate a message connected with the status of the individual or group: he who sacrifices most lavishly has the most to sacrifice, and is therefore worthy of the greatest honor. Sport also, and for the same reason, communicates a message concerning the individual's status: he who can run the fastest or throw the farthest or lift the most has the greatest amount of energy to sacrifice, and is therefore worthy of the greatest honor. He it is who marries the daughter of the king, or who becomes king himself.

But sport is not invariably competitive. Nor does sacrifice always serve to communicate status. The competitive aspects of sport and of other forms of sacrifice are secondary and are not essential to the message that is communicated, which is, in effect, "I am in possession of a surplus and I am aware that by giving up part or all of my surplus I will ensure the possession of a surplus in future." For it is a surplus of energy that enables sport to exist, and it is a surplus of material goods that makes possible other forms of sacrifice. Sport becomes competitive as readily as other forms of sacrifice, but competition is epiphenomenal. By recognizing the ritual and sacrificial nature of sport we can understand how it is that competition, which seems to many commentators to be a necessary component of sport, is merely secondary. Man does not run or throw in the first place for the purpose of demonstrating that he can run faster or throw farther. It is an easy enough task to find someone than whom one can run faster or throw farther; likewise it is not difficult to find someone by whom one can be surpassed in these endeavors. Rather, man runs and throws in order to demonstrate that, although he need do neither, he can run and throw. Those who, like Guttmann and Mandell, insist upon defining sport in terms of competition find that they must exclude entirely or relegate to a questionable status a number of activities that are usually regarded as sport and that clearly possess all the other characteristics of sport. Must we demand that hunting, bullfighting and mountain climbing be competitive in order to qualify as sport? Surely it is arbitrary to assert that the man who shoots at clay pigeons is engaged in an activity different in essence from that engaged in by the man who shoots at ducks.

By recognizing the sacrificial nature of sport, we not only solve the problem of whether sport must be competitive. Other concerns that have beset the study of sport can now also be seen to fade into the background. For example, it used to be thought that the observable professionalization of sport was leading to the demise of sport in the true sense of the word. It was felt that accepting remuneration for engaging in an activity that had been defined as something pursued "for its own sake" was paradoxical. By a clever argument Guttmann even seeks to show that professionalism is a logical extension of the ideals of sport as it had developed in the eighteenth and nineteenth centuries, inasmuch as professionalism ensures equality of opportunity for all participants.[120] But this sort of specious sophism is unnecessary, for professionalism is as irrelevant to the essence of sport as it is to the essence of any other endeavor. We do not assess a concerto composed by the amateur musician Frederick II of Prussia, for example, by a set of criteria different from those that we apply to one composed by the king's highly paid flute teacher, Johann Joachim Quantz, nor do we regard the two concertos as the products of activities that are in any fundamental sense distinct. The "problem" of professionalism in sport only arises when we insist upon defining sport as an autotelic activity.[121] The ends of sport lie outside itself, and can be achieved as well whether one is paid to achieve them or not. In some societies sacrifice is normally carried out by private individuals; in others it is the preserve of a professional priestly class. These are merely cultural differences that have no bearing on the essential nature of sacrifice. Related to the problem of professionalism is the question of the relationship between spectator and participant. It is often felt that the increase of professionalism relegates an increasing number of potential sportsmen to the status of "mere" spectators, and that this occurrence is contrary to the true nature of sport. Again, a value judgment is being made, based upon a definition of sport in terms of nineteenth-century British ideals. The rise of "spectator-sports" is no more a debasement of sport than the division of labor is a debasement of work. If sport is the ritual sacrifice of physical energy, it makes little difference whether I choose to engage personally in the ritual by demonstrating my superiority over a colleague on the tennis

120. Guttmann, *From Ritual to Record* 31–32.
121. See ibid. 3

court or observe as a deputation of semi-professional athletes displays on my behalf the amount of energy that my country is willing and able to squander at the Olympic Games.

But, if the professional athlete (as well as the athlete to whom it is now common to apply the adjective "amateur," quotation marks and all) is the priest sacrificing on my behalf, he is also, since it is his own energy that is being sacrificed, in a sense the sacrificial victim. And this leads us to consider two possible objections that may arise to our definition of sport. In the first place, does it make sense for sacrificer and victim to be one and the same? And, in the second place, does it make sense to speak of the "sacrifice" of something as incorporeal as human energy? In fact, as we shall see, neither of these phenomena is without parallel elsewhere in the realm of sacrifice. As far as the relationship between sacrificer and victim is concerned, it is a general feature of sacrifice that, even if the two are not identical, they are identified with each other as closely as possible. Before the sacrifice takes place, this identification is made in many instances by physical contact.

> This contact is obtained, in Semitic ritual, by the laying on of hands, and in others by equivalent rites. Through this proximity the victim, who already represents the gods, comes to represent the sacrifier also. Indeed, it is not enough to say that it represents him: it is merged in him. The two personalities are fused together.[122]

After the sacrifice has taken place, the identification is renewed by a variety of means,

> for example, the sprinkling of blood, the application of the skin of the victim, anointings with the fat, contact with the residue of the cremation. Sometimes the animal was cut into two parts and the sacrifier walked between them. But the most perfect way of effecting communication was to hand over to the sacrifier a portion of the victim, which he consumed. By eating a portion of it he assimilated to himself the characteristics of the whole.[123]

These are, of course, symbolic means of identifying victim and sacrificer. On a more concrete level, however, there are instances of sacrificers giving up themselves or parts of themselves. The phenomenon of

---

122. Hubert and Mauss, *Sacrifice* 32. The word *sacrifier* is here and in the following quotation used to refer to the person for whose benefit the sacrifice is performed.
123. Ibid. 39–40.

human self-sacrifice has recently been studied by H. S. Versnel, and a number of examples can be found in the pages of his excellent article.[124] It is also a common and widespread custom to offer up parts of the body as a sacrifice to the gods or to the spirits of the dead. We have already noted Achilles' offering of a lock of hair to the spirit of the dead Patroclus: while Patroclus still lived, Achilles intended the hair to serve as a dedication to the river Spercheius.[125] Similarly, Orestes dedicates one lock of his hair to Inachus, and a second to his deceased father, Agamemnon.[126] The Nazirite offers his hair to Yahweh, just as girls in ancient Greece dedicated theirs to Artemis on attaining puberty.[127] Another ritual practice in which a part of the body is removed is the custom of circumcision, which is observed by the Jews, the Moslems, the ancient Egyptians and a number of other peoples of Africa and Australia.[128] Somewhat more radical is the practice of self-castration, which was engaged in by the Phrygian Galloi.[129] The Brahmin can even speak of the fat that he has caused to disappear by fasting as having been "sacrificed."[130] Under the rather quaint heading "Austerities," the *Hastings Encyclopaedia of Religion and Ethics* refers to similar customs among the peoples of six continents, as well as the customs of amputating fingers and knocking out teeth.[131] As we have already noted, it is likely that these practices, as well as other forms of ritual mutilation and laceration, derive from original and spontaneous reactions to bereavement.[132] But they have developed into forms of sacrifice. A part of the body is given up, or the body is itself somehow impaired, so that, paradoxically, the body is strengthened. Just so wine is poured upon the ground so that there may be more wine, and a sheep is destroyed so that the flock may increase. The Cherokee's self-mutilation and his ritual expenditure of energy in the ball game are alternative forms of sacrifice,

---

124. H. S. Versnel, "Self-Sacrifice, Compensation and the Anonymous Gods," *Entretiens sur l'antiquité classique* 27 (1980) 135–85.

125. *Iliad* 23.141–42.

126. Aeschylus, *The Libation Bearers* 6–7; cf. Euripides, *Iphigeneia among the Taurians* 174, *Alcestis* 101, *Electra* 515.

127. Numbers 6.5–19; Gaster, *Myth, Legend, and Custom in the Old Testament* 438. For hair-offerings, see Meuli, "Griechische Opferbräuche" 205 n. 1 (= *Gesammelte Schriften* II 928 n. 2).

128. E.g., Frazer, *Taboo* 156, 227, 244.

129. Frazer, *Magic Art* II 144–45; Burkert, *Structure* 120.

130. Hubert and Mauss, *Sacrifice* 21 with n. 66.

131. J. Hastings, ed., *Encyclopaedia of Religion and Ethics* II (Edinburgh, 1913) 232–34. Cf. also G. Majno, *The Healing Hand: Man and Wound in the Ancient World* (Cambridge, Mass., 1975) 19–21.

132. Meuli, "Griechische Opferbräuche" 203ff. (= *Gesammelte Schriften* II 926ff.).

just as Achilles' dedication of a lock of hair and his ritual destruction of valuable horses are alternative forms of sacrifice. Giving up part or all of oneself and giving up part or all of one's property are parallel activities and are capable of serving the same purpose.

Thus there can be no objection to our definition of sport on the grounds that it is impossible or irrational for sacrificer and victim to be one and the same. Now we must address ourselves to the other potential objection, namely that, since physical energy is incorporeal, it cannot be "sacrificed." To begin with, there is no reason to believe that the concept of incorporeality even exists among primitive peoples. A recent study has shown that the concept did not arise until the fourth century B.C. and probably originated in the philosophy of Plato.[133] To speak of energy, life-force, soul, as "incorporeal" for the peoples among whom sacrifice originated is to commit an anachronism. In his remarkable book *The Origins of European Thought*, R. B. Onians points out that even among the ancient Greeks and Romans, a man's strength and life-force were conceived of in very concrete terms.[134] In particular, they are spoken of as though they were a liquid that resides in the body and that can be conserved, expended and replenished. Nor is this conception of human energy confined to the Greeks and Romans. Onians includes comparative material from elsewhere as well, and, indeed, even we use the expression "elbow grease" to refer to vigorous physical effort. Originally elbow grease meant "sweat," and

> sweat would naturally seem to be the stuff of strength, vigour, since it is expended when strength, vigour, is expended, and conversely he who sweats through external heat feels loss of strength, of vigour. The Nubians suppose it will give them strength to apply the sweat of their horses to their own bodies. In the Torres Straits men drink the sweat of famous warriors in the belief that in it they are getting their valour.[135]

Human energy can also be identified with other bodily fluids. The observed lassitude of men following ejaculation leads to the belief that one's strength is reduced as a result of the loss of semen and to the consequent identification of semen and strength.[136] Saliva also is identified with strength and, inasmuch as it is occasionally considered to be

133. R. Renehan, "On the Greek Origins of the Concepts Incorporeality and Immateriality," *Greek, Roman, and Byzantine Studies* 21 (1980) 105–38.
134. Onians, *Origins of European Thought* 187–228.
135. Ibid. 191.
136. Ibid.

capable of bringing about impregnation, is in turn identified with semen.[137] Saliva is felt to have curative powers and the power to increase
the strength of one who is anointed with it. For example, Jesus cures
blindness by spitting into the eyes of a blind man or by smearing mud,
made by spitting on the ground, on his eyes.[138] Even today it is not
uncommon to see someone spitting into his palm before beginning a
heavy task. This practice was noticed as long ago as the first century by
Pliny, who explains it as a means of increasing the force of a blow. As
Frank W. Nicolson points out,

> this seems rather a far-fetched explanation of the reason why
> spade-laborers, for instance, spit constantly upon their hands.
> One would naturally say that the explanation was purely a
> physical one,—they spit to moisten the hand and so secure a
> firmer grasp of the implement they are using. Yet there are cases
> where the action seems purely symbolical, as, for instance, when
> a man dares another to "come on," and by way of preparation,
> and of enforcing the power of his blows, "rolls up his sleeves
> and spits on his hands."[139]

Nicolson might have noted further that there is no reason for spade
laborers to moisten their hands, since their work causes them to per-
spire freely. I would suggest that the practice is designed precisely to
replenish the strength perceived to be in danger of being lost through
perspiration.

Very likely the therapeutic value of saliva helped to influence the
notion that the application of saliva can increase strength. This is presumably the reason that the Huichol Indians of Mexico, as part of their
preparation for hunting deer, would spit on their palms "and then rub
them quickly over their joints, legs, and shoulders."[140] Likewise the
Zuñi Indians of New Mexico would prepare for a ball race by chewing
a piece of root, spitting it out into their hands and rubbing it over their
bodies.[141] And, after their ordeal of scratching, the Cherokees would
similarly chew a root and spit out the juice over their bodies.[142] These

137. E.g., Frazer, *Taboo* 387; E. S. Hartland, *Primitive Paternity: The Myth of Supernatural Birth in Relation to the History of the Family* I (London, 1909) 12, 18, 19, 68, 70.
138. Mark 8.23, John 9.6. See further C. de Mensignac, *Recherches ethnographiques
sur la salive et le crachat* (Bordeaux, 1892).
139. "The Saliva Superstition in Classical Literature," *Harvard Studies in Classical
Philology* 8 (1897) 34. Cf. Eibl-Eibesfeldt, *Love and Hate* 56.
140. Frazer, *Taboo* 197.
141. Culin, *Games of the North American Indians* 693.
142. Mooney, "Cherokee Ball-Play" 122 (= Culin, *Games of the North American
Indians* 581).

fluids, then—semen, saliva, sweat—are identified in primitive thought with the life-force and with strength. When they are expended, strength is diminished; when they are replenished, strength is restored. Strength can also be restored by the application to the body of other fluids. When one is exercising and perspiring, one is restored by a bath or a shower. The apparent (but not the correct) explanation for this is that the water has replaced the fluid lost by the body. Thus a bath or shower *before* exertion can strengthen the body by infusing a surplus of fluid, just as the application of saliva can strengthen the limbs before hunting or before a game. Other fluids as well, particularly fats and oils, can perform the same function.[143] And, indeed, these substances are frequently employed by hunters and athletes for anointing the body.

But there is another, and perhaps more important, reason for the hunter to engage in these practices. Before the hunter goes out in quest of his prey, he does whatever he can to prevent the animal from catching his scent and, hence, from being scared away. And so the hunter bathes. He puts on clean clothes; that is to say, he puts on clothes that have not yet been imbued with his scent. He fumigates his body by leaping over or dancing around a fire into which aromatics have been cast. He anoints his body with animal fats or with aromatic oils. He may even dress himself in animal skins in order to disguise himself from his prey, as the Eskimo wears a sealskin so as to get closer to the herd.[144] All these things he does for very good, very pragmatic, reasons. Another precaution that the primitive hunter takes for similarly pragmatic reasons is that he refrains, as we have seen above, from sexual intercourse. He does this because he fears (wrongly, as it turns out) that intercourse will diminish his strength and his chances for success on the hunt.

We are now in a position to understand why sexual intercourse has been regarded as shameful. There is, after all, nothing inherently shameful, unclean or impure about intercourse. On the contrary, as the process whereby human life is created, it ought to lay claim to a very different status, as being beautiful, sacred and pure. But by a sheer accident of human history it has become associated with that which is unclean. The primitive hunter abstained from intercourse for the same reason he bathed his body, namely to ensure that he be successful on the hunt. For reasons that have nothing to do either with bathing or with inter-

---

143. Onians, *Origins of European Thought* 188–89, 210–12.
144. K. Birket-Smith, *The Eskimos,* revised English translation (London, 1959) 79. This is the trick that Menelaus employed to catch the Old Man of the Sea (*Odyssey* 4.435–55).

course, the entire hunting ritual became transformed, in the course of history, into sacrificial ritual. The idea of the sacred arose, and the gods sprang into being to serve, among other things, as the recipients of sacrificial offerings. Because the hunter had practiced continence before the hunt, had bathed and changed his clothes, had fumigated his body and anointed it, the priest did the same before sacrificing. And, since the sacrifice was now felt to be performed for the purpose of pleasing and benefiting the god, all of the various elements of the ritual must be explained as conforming to the wishes of the god. And so the god approves of cleanliness (which is, after all, according to the proverb, "next to godliness") and frowns upon sexual intercourse. Intercourse is not unclean; rather, the association that I have just sketched, which has been ingrained through countless generations of ritual practice, has caused it to be felt as such.

I began this essay with the observation that there is no equivalent for the word *sport* in other languages, and that, for this reason, the English word has been widely adopted by the speakers of a number of languages throughout the world. I noted also that the fact of the word's relatively recent restriction in meaning seems to support the view that the phenomenon to which it refers is likewise a relatively recent development. But I have since defined sport as a form of ritual sacrifice and have shown that its origins are to be sought in mankind's most distant and nearly irrecoverable past. How is the antiquity of the phenomenon compatible with the novelty of the term? In fact, there is an exact parallel in the case of the word *sacrifice*. For neither ancient Greek nor Hebrew has an equivalent to the English word,[145] despite the fact that the familiarity of the Greeks and the Jews with the practice is undeniable. Both languages have words that designate specific kinds of sacrifice, such as burnt offerings, libations and the like, but neither has a general term that corresponds to our word. In fact, the word derives from a rather vague Latin expression that means something like "the act of consecrating or rendering sacred by offering to a deity." Likewise, while Greek has terms that refer to specific kinds of sporting events, like athletics or equestrian events, it has no general or inclusive term. The only word that a Greek could use that would embrace both athletic and equestrian sports, both of which were represented at the Olympic Games, is a general word that means "contests," which can also desig-

---

145. R. K. Yerkes, *Sacrifice in Greek and Roman Religions and Early Judaism* (New York, 1952) 6–7.

nate musical competitions, military encounters and actions at law. Thus it is not legitimate to use the fact that the ancient Greeks, for example, had no word corresponding to our word *sport* as evidence that the activities engaged in today and designated by the word *sport* are fundamentally different from those similar activities engaged in by the ancient Greeks.

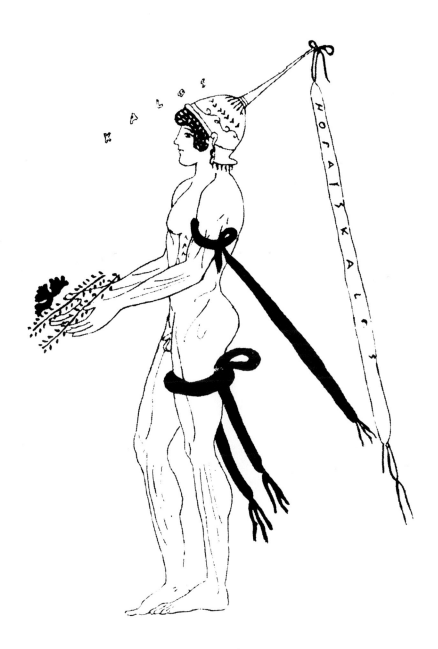

Figure 1 Victorious athlete holding branches
and wearing fillets. Detail of red-figure am-
phora by Douris. Early fifth century B.C.

Figure 2　An official binding a fillet on the
head of a victorious athlete, who is holding
branches and wearing fillets on his arm and
leg. Detail of red-figure hydria. Early fifth century B.C.

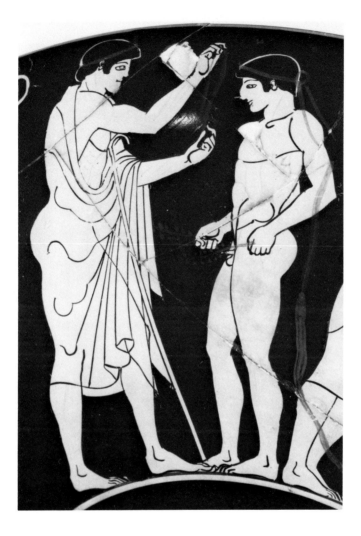

Figure 3 Victorious athlete holding branches
and having fillets tied around his head. Detail
of red-figure drinking cup by Douris. Early
fifth century B.C.

Figure 4   Victorious athlete holding branches
and having fillets tied around his head. Interior
of red-figure drinking cup by the Ashby
Painter. Early fifth century B.C.

Figure 5 Australian aborigines hunting kangaroo; one hides behind a portable screen of leaves. Engraving from J. G. Wood, *The Natural History of Man*.

Figure 6   Victorious athlete holding branches
and wearing fillets. Interior of red-figure drinking cup by the Tarquinia Painter. Mid fifth
century B.C.

Figure 7 Australian aborigines hunting kangaroo, using screens and headdresses made of brush. Native drawing made in 1876.

Figure 8 Athletes wearing crowns of vegetation. Detail of red-figure drinking cup in the
manner of the Epeleios Painter. Early fifth century B.C.

Figure 9 Australian aborigines hunting emu;
one holds a portable screen of leaves and wears
a leafy headdress. Engraving from E. Delessert,
*Voyages dans les deux océans. Atlantique et
Pacifique.*

Figure 10 Winged Victory watering sacrificial
bull (wearing fillets) in front of tripod; woman
about to tie additional fillets on bull. Detail of
red-figure stamnos by the Hector Painter. Mid
fifth century B.C.

Figure 11   Winged Victory binding fillet on
victor in the torch race; priest with crown of
vegetation standing behind altar. Detail of red- .
figure krater by the Nikias Painter. Late fifth
century B.C.

Figure 12   Discus thrower with prize tripod
in the background. Silver coin from Cos. Fifth
century B.C.

Figure 13   Bronze cauldron found at Cyme in
Italy, inscribed, "I was set out as a prize at the
games of Onomastus, son of Pheidilaus." Sixth
century B.C.

Figure 14 Wrestlers with prize cauldrons in the background. Detail of wall painting from the Tomb of the Augurs, Tarquinia (Italy). Late fifth century B.C.

Figure 15 Chariot race at the funeral games for Patroclus, with prize tripod in the background. Detail of black-figure krater by Kleitias and Ergotimos (the "François vase"). Early sixth century B.C.

Figure 16 Boxers with prize tripod in the
background. Fragment of black-figure vase.
Mid sixth century B.C.

Figure 17 Ram being led to the altar for sacrifice to the accompaniment of a double pipe (*aulos*). Detail of red-figure krater in the manner of the Kleophon Painter. Late fifth century B.C.

Figure 18 Boxing instruction accompanied by
the double pipe (*aulos*). Detail of black-figure
pelike by the Acheloos Painter. Late sixth century B.C.

Figure 19 Sacrificial meat being roasted at the
altar to the accompaniment of a double pipe
(*aulos*). Detail of red-figure stamnos by Poly-
gnotos. Mid fifth century B.C.

Figure 20   Athletes accompanied by a double-
pipe (*aulos*) player. Detail of red-figure krater
by the Troilos Painter. Early fifth century B.C.

Figure 21   Bull being led to the altar for sacrifice to the accompaniment of a double pipe
(*aulos*). Black-figure lekanis. Mid sixth century
B.C.

Figure 22 Long jumpers accompanied by a
double-pipe (*aulos*) player. Detail of red-figure
drinking cup by Douris. Early fifth century
B.C.

Figure 23 Infibulated boxers and javelin
thrower. Detail of wall painting from the
Tomb of the Monkey, Chiusi (Italy). Early
fifth century B.C.

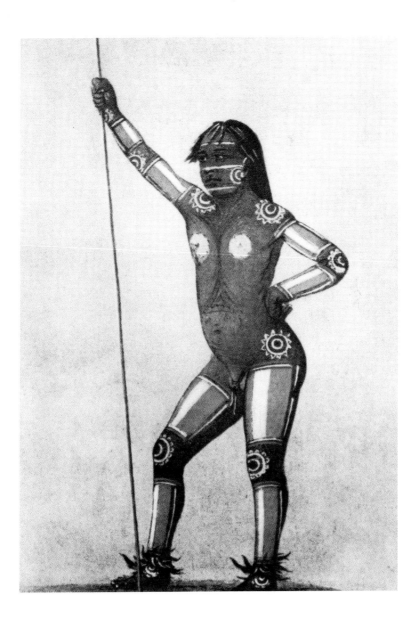

Figure 24   Infibulated and painted Mandan
Indian, prepared to participate in the bull-
dance. Reproduced from George Catlin,
O-Kee-Pa.

Figure 25 Trainer handing strigil to young
man, who is coming from music lesson. Red-
figure skyphos by the Lewis Painter. Mid fifth
century B.C.

Part Two

The Nature of Greek Athletics

In Part One, I presented the case for a new definition of sport, namely, that it is a ritual sacrifice of human energy. The evidence used in support of that definition comes from a wide variety of cultures, from the most primitive tribal societies to our own presumably advanced civilization, and the impression may be given that it has been deliberately selected from the vast repertory of observed human behavior in such a way as to prejudice the case. In Part Two, I shall examine in some detail the sport of the ancient Greeks in the light of this definition. There are several reasons for adopting this procedure. To begin with, it is worth while focusing on the sport of one society in order to counteract the impression mentioned above, that the evidence has been selectively presented. If I can demonstrate—as I believe I can—that sport in ancient Greece was indeed a ritual sacrifice of human energy, then there will be a strong presumption, particularly given the nature of ritual behavior, that the same definition ought to be applied to sport in other societies as well. At any rate, it will rest with others to show that there is a fundamental difference between sport in ancient Greece and, say, sport today. And, again given the nature of ritual behavior, that will be no easy task. It has been felt best to avoid using sport in our own society as a test case, partly because the evidence available is so considerable that it would be impossible to treat it adequately in brief compass, partly because of the hypermetropia that afflicts us whenever we consider human behavior. We more readily admit the truth of assertions made about societies other than our own.

Ancient Greece has been chosen in large measure for purely pragmatic reasons. As a classical scholar, I am simply more familiar with the
sport of the Greeks than with that of any other society (excepting, of
course, my own). But there are more compelling reasons for including
a discussion of ancient Greek sport here. We possess more complete
documentation for sport, and for the attitude toward sport, among the
ancient Greeks than we do for any society other than our own. And
that documentation is of a remarkable, even unique, sort. For the ancient Greeks occupy a special place in the history of human civilization.
It is universally acknowledged that the Greeks, from the time of Homer
to that of Plutarch and beyond, were extraordinarily successful in articu-
lating the fundamental aspects of human experience, not only in their
enormously original and influential literature, but also in the visual arts
and in the myths and cults with which we are familiar primarily from
literary sources, but which represent the collective and anonymous expression of the Greek people. But in addition to their signal articulate-
ness, the Greeks also display certain affinities with the "primitive," often
denied by those who would idealize the Greeks but stressed by Nietzsche and by E. R. Dodds in his brilliant book, *The Greeks and the Irrational*.[1] Thus the Greeks are in a unique mediatory position; they were
capable of experiencing what is at the root of human feeling and con-
sciousness, and they communicate it to us in terms that are familiar to
us (partly because we have inherited them from the Greeks). It is for
this reason that the myths and literature of the Greeks have exercised so
great an influence on the ideas of such original and important thinkers
as Friedrich Nietzsche, Sigmund Freud and James Frazer.

When we consider sport in ancient Greece, the first thing that strikes
us is the remarkable importance that sport assumed in the life and
thought of the Greeks. To a certain degree, this is simply a reflection of
the singularly competitive character of the Greeks, who were not only
avid participants in athletic contests but also regularly held competitions in, for example, dancing, lyre playing and drinking. The great
plays of Aeschylus, Sophocles, Euripides and Aristophanes, which are
among the masterpieces of Western dramatic literature, were all produced for the first time in Athens as entries in a competition for the
writing of tragedies and comedies. An inscription seems to tell us that
the sculptor Paeonius won the right to design the akroteria of the
Temple of Zeus at Olympia as the result of a victory in some sort of

1. E. R. Dodds, *The Greeks and the Irrational* (Berkeley, 1951).

artistic competition.[2] In a society as competitive as that of the ancient Greeks, it is not surprising that sports, particularly competitive sports, were very popular. But it is not just the popularity of Greek sports that is striking. After all, gladiatorial combats and chariot racing had enormous popular appeal in ancient Rome, and soccer is no less popular throughout the world today. What is remarkable about Greek sport is the seriousness with which it was taken as a cultural and even religious phenomenon. Serious thinkers and writers in ancient Rome tended to scorn the Circus and avoid the arena, just as intellectuals today despise, or affect to despise, popular sport. But in ancient Greece the story was different. It is not unusual for a dramatist like Aeschylus to draw his metaphors, or for a philosopher like Plato to select his illustrations, from the realms of chariot racing or wrestling. Indeed, in the hands of the most distinguished poets and artists, sport becomes itself the subject of great art. Everyone is familiar, for example, with Myron's statue of a discus thrower. And the famous bronze charioteer from Delphi was part of a dedicatory offering commissioned to celebrate a victory in the chariot race at the Pythian Games by Polyzalus, the tyrant of the Sicilian city of Gela. The most famous work of the great fourth-century artist Lysippus, the court sculptor to Alexander the Great, was a statue of an athlete scraping olive oil off his body following exercise, the so-called Apoxyomenos, copies of which still survive today. Now, it is not difficult for us to understand the connection between athletics and the visual arts; we are familiar with the acrobats of Picasso, the scenes of bullfighting in Goya, the photographic experiments of Eadweard Muybridge. (Although it is interesting to note that modern artists like Degas prefer dancers to acrobats, and that only Tait McKenzie has made a reputation based upon representations of figures from sport.)

We find it much harder to accept the fact that sport plays so great a rôle in Greek literature. The reason is that we tend to regard sport and literature as belonging to very different levels of experience: one is a part of our serious cultural life, the other is merely a form of entertainment or recreation. But for the ancient Greeks, clearly no such distinction existed. Greek literature may be said to begin with the *Iliad* of Homer, who did not feel it inappropriate to devote one of the twenty-four books (book 23) of his epic poem to a full and exciting account of the athletic contests held at the funeral of Patroclus. And the reputation

2. W. Dittenberger and K. Purgold, *Die Inschriften von Olympia* (Berlin, 1896) 377–84, no. 259.

of Pindar, who is considered by many scholars to be the finest and most
sublime of all Greek lyric poets, rests upon the four surviving books of
poems that he wrote on commission to celebrate victories won by various boxers, wrestlers, runners and owners of horses in the Olympic
Games and in the other so-called Panhellenic Games. The poetry of
Pindar has always been a puzzle to modern commentators, who are
surprised at the disparity between the weight of Pindar's diction and
the apparent triviality of his subject matter. It is sometimes even felt
that evidence can be found of Pindar's own awareness of this disparity
in the fact that he devotes so little of his time to the actual praise of the
athletic victors and so much of it to mythological excursuses, to moral-
istic sermonizing, and to disquisitions on the beatific state of the victor's
home town. But no one who reads Pindar without prejudice can doubt
his basic seriousness, and no one can deny his sincerity when he praises
victors in athletic contests as embodiments of *aretē* (a conception of
human excellence that implies moral worth as well as success and such
virtues as physical beauty, strength and courage) and when he speaks of
them in the same breath as gods and heroes. Nor is Pindar alone in this.
For other poets as well composed choral lyrics in praise of victors in
the games (although only those of Pindar and fragments of those of
Bacchylides have survived for us to read). And we must assume that
such a genre could not have arisen and flourished if the Greeks had not
felt it appropriate to devote serious poetry to the praise of athletic
victors.

We would not consider it appropriate for, say, T. S. Eliot to have
composed a formal ode celebrating the victory of the Saint Louis base-
ball team in the World Series. Therefore we feel it necessary to explain,
or to explain away, the practice of Pindar and his fellow composers of
epinician odes. The most successful attempt at explanation has been
made by Hermann Fränkel, the author of the most sensitive analysis of
Pindar's thought. According to Fränkel, Pindar and his contemporaries
believed that "all values by their very essence are of one and the same
nature," and that human value, or *aretē*, "is a unitary whole."

> It is only in this way that we can understand the high value that
> Pindar and his world set upon victories in the games. They
> thought not in terms of a specialized technical ability, but in
> terms of the demonstration, in this particular way, of the worth
> of an individual. If a man throws all that he has to give into
> pursuing a wholly ideal end: if he gives up his time and money,
> if he takes the risk of defeat and disgrace, if he undergoes the
> long and severe discipline of training with all its pains and pri-

> vations and efforts, and puts out every ounce of his strength in
> the event itself; and if then the grace of the gods, without which
> no achievement is possible, chooses him as victor from all his
> competitors, then in Pindar's eyes he has given convincing
> proof of his *aretē*.[3]

Everything that Fränkel says here is true and valuable, and we should
take particular note of his emphasis on the sacrifices made by the
victorious athlete in the pursuit of his goal. (In fact, what the English version renders as "gives up" is, in the original German, *opfert*—
"sacrifices" or "offers up.") But Fränkel does not thereby explain why
the Greeks did not feel it appropriate to honor in the same way those
who display *aretē* in some other pursuit. For there are no choral odes
in praise of philosophers or victorious military commanders. In reality,
the epinician odes of Pindar and Bacchylides are formal hymns sung in
praise of a god, Zeus in the case of the Olympic Games, Apollo in the
case of the Pythian Games, and so on. The fact that the victories celebrated in the hymns were won in contests that were actually part of a
religious festival is usually felt to be a sufficient justification for the custom of composing such hymns. But this is merely to explain by means
of putting the question in different terms. For the question still remains: Why are athletic contests felt to be appropriate components of a
religious festival?

This is a question already answered in Part One: Sport is, no less than
burnt offerings and libations, a form of ritual sacrifice. And this definition of sport is confirmed for us by examining sport in ancient Greece.
For the Greeks, in their literature and in their ritual practice, acknowledge the rôle of the athlete as sacrificial victim. It is this status that
entitles the athlete to so prominent a place in the hymns composed to
honor the gods. For the victim dedicated to the god must be, and must
be recognized as, the best of its kind. And so the finest of flock or herd
is singled out for sacrifice to the god. Agamemnon vowed to sacrifice
to Artemis "the finest thing born in the course of the year" (it turned
out to be his daughter).[4] Polycrates, the tyrant of Samos, was advised
to give up "that which is most valuable and which will be most grievous
to lose."[5] When Macaria offers to sacrifice herself in order to secure
victory in war, she is assured that she is the most outstanding of all

---

3. H. Fränkel, *Early Greek Poetry and Philosophy,* English translation (Oxford, 1975)
487–88.
4. Euripides, *Iphigeneia among the Taurians* 20–21.
5. Herodotus, *Histories* 3.40.4.

women for courage and that she will be honored above all.[6] The god must be given a worthy gift; he will feel slighted if he is not given the best. The athletic contest performs two functions at the same time. In the first place, it is, in itself, the means whereby the sacrifice of human energy takes place. Among the Timbira Indians, and in many other societies, this is its primary, or even sole, function: everyone who participates in the contest is felt to have sacrificed; winning or losing is not, as they say, as important as having taken part. But for the Greeks the contest performed a second function as well. By testing to see who could run the fastest or throw the farthest, it determined who was considered to be worthy of sacrificing to the god. For the losers were embarrassed and ashamed. Pindar pictures them as cowering in back alleys, hiding from their enemies, smitten with disgrace.[7] Only the victor was dedicated to the god.

Nor is this merely a figure of speech. The ritual connected with victory in the games indicates clearly and unambiguously that the victorious athlete was indeed dedicated to the god. One aspect of that ritual for which we have a great deal of evidence is that, following his victory, the athlete was decorated with woolen fillets.[8] For example, Pindar concludes his Fifth Isthmian Ode by exhorting the Muse to

> Take a wreath for him [i.e., the victor], and bring
> A head-band of soft wool,
> And with them send this new song on its wings.

These fillets were so commonly associated with victory in athletic contests that Thucydides says that, on one occasion, the people of Scione welcomed the Spartan general Brasidas so enthusiastically that "they publicly crowned him with a golden crown as the liberator of Greece and private citizens would come up to him and place fillets on him as though he were an athlete."[9] In a similar passage, Plutarch tells us that, after Pericles had delivered his famous funeral oration in honor of those who had died in the first year of the Peloponnesian War, the women "crowned him with wreaths and fillets as though he were a victorious athlete."[10] And, indeed, there are numerous references in Greek lit-

---

6. Euripides, *Children of Heracles* 597–99.

7. Pindar, *Pythian Odes* 8.90–91. The translation below is by C. M. Bowra (Harmondsworth, 1969).

8. For these fillets, see J. Servais in *L'Antiquité Classique* 36 (1967) 415–56.

9. Thucydides, *The Peloponnesian War* 4.121.1.

10. Plutarch, *Life of Pericles* 28.5; cf. Cornelius Nepos, *Life of Alcibiades* 6.3.

erature to this practice of binding woolen fillets onto victors in the games.[11] There are also several representations on painted vases of victorious athletes so decorated. For example, on a red-figure vase in the Hermitage Museum, Leningrad, there is a victorious athlete wearing a helmet and holding branches in his hands. His upper arm and his thigh have purple woolen bands tied around them (Fig. 1). A victorious runner is similarly depicted on a red-figure vase in the Antikensammlungen in Munich. He too is holding branches and has woolen bands tied about his arm and leg; an official of the games is in the process of tying a fillet about his head (Fig. 2). Similar scenes are shown on three red-figure drinking cups, one in the British Museum, one in the Bibliothèque Nationale, and one that was formerly in the Raifé collection but whose present location is unknown (Figs. 3, 4, 6).

The purpose of these woolen fillets is to signify the consecration of the victor to the god. Just so, the priest or the priestess wears fillets to indicate that he or she belongs to, and is devoted to, the god. In Aeschylus' *Agamemnon,* before Cassandra goes to her death, she indicates the termination of her priestly service to Apollo by throwing her scepter and fillets to the ground.[12] The priest of Zeus at Pergamon was required to wear "a white mantle and a crown of olive with a purple fillet."[13] The person who held the ceremonial position of torch-bearer at the Eleusinian mysteries traditionally wore fillets in his hair.[14] (These fillets survive today as the infulae attached to the mitres of Roman Catholic bishops.) It is not only the priest or the servant of the god who signifies his devotion to the god by the wearing of fillets; the sacrificial victim, that which is most conspicuously dedicated to the god, is also so decorated. In Aristophanes' *Peace,* Trygaeus indicates that the sacrifice is ready by saying, "here is the basket containing the grain [for strewing on the victim] and the fillet and the knife."[15] In order to display to the world that he has sacrificed an ox, the man in Theophrastus who is afflicted with feelings of petty pride nails up the forepart of the victim's skull opposite the entrance to his house "bound about with large fillets."[16] And Lucian tells us explicitly that it was customary to tie

11. E.g., Thucydides, *The Peloponnesian War* 5.50.4; Pausanias, *Description of Greece* 6.1.7, 6.2.2, 6.20.19.

12. Aeschylus, *Agamemnon* 1264–65.

13. W. Dittenberger, *Sylloge inscriptionum Graecarum,* third edition, III (Leipzig, 1920) 161, no. 1018.

14. Plutarch, *Life of Aristeides* 5.7.

15. Aristophanes, *Peace* 948.

16. Theophrastus, *Characters* 21.7.

fillets about sacrificial victims before they were sacrificed.[17] This is borne out by representations of sacrifice in the visual arts. A fifth-century painting, for example, on a red-figure wine jar in Munich shows a scene in which a winged Victory is giving an ox a drink of water preparatory to sacrifice; the ox wears a white fillet in its horns and is about to be further decorated with fillets (Fig. 10). And similarly, on the rare occasions when human sacrifice is referred to, fillets are usually mentioned. When Macaria offers herself for sacrifice in Euripides' *Children of Heracles* she says, "Lead me to the place where it is necessary for me to die and bind me with fillets."[18] In a portion of *Iphigeneia in Aulis* not, it is true, written by Euripides, but dating from the third or fourth century B.C., we are told that Calchas, who presided over the sacrifice of Iphigeneia, "crowned the head of the maiden."[19] And Herodotus tells us of a peculiar custom of the people of the town of Alus in Achaea: the members of a certain family were forbidden to enter the town hall; if they were caught doing so, they were "decked with fillets, led out in a procession and sacrificed."[20]

Thus the woolen fillet was the mark both of the sacrificer and the victim, and we have seen that the victorious athlete combines both these functions. The material of which these fillets were made was symbolic of this dual function. For the woolen bands worn by priest and victim alike were the last vestige of the primitive hunting practice of dressing up in the hide of the victim.[21] Certain other features of Greek athletic practice were also symbolic of this dual function. At the ancient Olympic Games the most important event was the one-stade footrace. This was a race of one length of the stadium (six hundred feet), of which the starting line was at the far end and the finish line at the end nearest to the altar of Zeus. In fact, the stadium at Olympia was originally constructed in such a way that the finish line was directly in front of the altar. In other words, the one-stade race was a race from some point outside the sacred precinct of the god to the altar of the god. Now, in

17. Lucian, *On Sacrifices* 12; cf. Plutarch, *Life of Aemilius Paullus* 33.2; Acts of the Apostles 14.13.

18. Euripides, *Children of Heracles* 528–29.

19. Euripides, *Iphigeneia in Aulis* 1567. For the date of this portion of the play, see the *Bulletin of the Institute of Classical Studies* (London) 28 (1981) 74.

20. Herodotus, *Histories* 7.197.2.

21. Burkert, *Greek Religion* 235–36. According to Ludwig Drees, the fillets at the Olympic Games symbolize the ram of Pelops (*Der Ursprung der Olympischen Spiele,* Beiträge zur Lehre und Forschung der Leibeserziehung 13 [Schorndorf bei Stuttgart, 1962] 86).

sacrificial ritual, it is of considerable importance that the victim be (or at least give the impression of being) willingly led to the altar.[22] In the case of the one-stade race, there was an actual contest to see who could reach the altar first. There can be no greater sign of willingness than the athlete's expenditure of every effort to reach the altar before anyone else. In virtue of his willingness and of his expenditure of energy, the athlete is the sacrificial victim. But his rôle as sacrificer is also acknowledged symbolically. For, in the classical period, the footraces took place on the central day of the five-day festival, the day on which the great sacrifice was made to Olympian Zeus. According to Philostratus, the victim, an ox, was slaughtered and, following the usual sacrificial practice, the consecrated parts of the victim were placed on the altar. Then the race was held, and the victor lit the fire in which the consecrated parts were burned up. This practice has parallels elsewhere in the Greek world. A race was held at Delphi, the goal of which was the altar and the winner of which also ignited the fire on the altar.[23] Many Greek cities also held torch races in connection with various religious festivals. In most instances these were relay races, in which the members of each team took turns carrying the torch toward the goal, which was in each case the altar of some god or goddess.[24] On a vase painting in the British Museum, the finish of such a race is depicted (Fig. 11). On one side of the altar is the priest; on the other is the victor in the race. He is attended by a winged Victory who is about to place a fillet on him as he is in the process of lighting the fire on the altar.

This painting also illustrates another feature that is characteristic of Greek athletics. The victorious athlete, like the priest (and, indeed, like the figure of Victory herself), is crowned. The particular crown that he wears is unusual, and is depicted only in connection with the torch race. Unfortunately, the evidence that we have available to us does not allow us to decide whether the crown was worn by all the participants in the race or was conferred only upon the victors at the end of the race. The literary sources are silent, and the vase paintings sometimes show the runners competing in the race with crowns and sometimes without. Perhaps different customs were observed in different cities. Nor can we be more precise about the nature of the crown itself. Scholars are not agreed as to whether the spikes of the crown were leaves or feath-

22. Burkert, *Homo Necans* 3–4; *Greek Religion* 56.
23. Burkert, *Homo Necans* 97, citing Philostratus, *On Gymnastics* 5, and, for Delphi, F. Sokolowski, *Lois sacrées des cités grecques: Supplément* (Paris, 1962) 90, no. 44.15.
24. Weiler, *Der Sport* 155–56.

ers, but comparison with other athletic events in ancient Greece ought to incline us to the former view. For it was the regular practice to crown victorious athletes with (fillets and) crowns of vegetation.[25] These crowns took a variety of forms, depending upon the location of the contest in which they were awarded and upon the god in whose honor the contest was held. In the case of the torch race, it is reasonable to assume that the shape of the crown was intended to be symbolic of the flame of the torch. But the fact that the victor wore a crown at all is symbolic of his sacerdotal function, which he usurped from the priest, of lighting the sacrificial fire. For a crown of vegetation was worn by the priest as well as by the victorious athlete. We referred above to the requirement that the priest of Zeus at Pergamon wear a crown of olive.[26] The priest or priestess of Artemis wore a crown of laurel.[27] And representations of scenes of sacrifice on painted vases regularly show the priest presiding over the sacrifice as wearing a crown of leaves of some kind.[28]

What the original function of the crown of vegetation was has not been determined with any certainty.[29] We do know, however, that it was, like the fillets, a mark of that which was dedicated to the god. In Aristophanes' *Peace,* when Trygaeus is about to conduct a sacrifice, he says to his servant, "Do a good job of roasting the victim, for here comes someone who is crowned with laurel."[30] The ancient commentator, or scholiast, on this line explains the statement by pointing out that "priests and prophets were crowned with laurel as a symbol of their craft." So it is clear that a crown of vegetation was worn by the priest and by the victorious athlete because both were conceived of as dedicated to the god. But what is the connection between the crown on the one hand and the priest and the athlete on the other? Onians emphasizes the shape of the crown and considers it in its function as *binding* the head.[31] He does not distinguish between the crown of vegetation and the woolen fillets that were also bound around the head (as well as about the arms and legs, as we have seen). But it is important to distinguish between crowns and fillets, not only because of the difference in

25. For details and further illustrations, see G. Q. Giglioli, "Phyllobolia," *Archeologia classica* 2 (1950) 31–45.

26. See above, p. 81, n. 13.

27. Heliodorus, *Aethiopica* 1.2; Achilles Tatius, *Leucippe and Cleitophon* 7.12.2.

28. See, for example, Figs. 11, 17 and 19.

29. See K. Baus, *Der Kranz in Antike und Christentum* (Bonn, 1940).

30. Aristophanes, *Peace* 1043–44.

31. Onians, *Origins of European Thought* 376–77.

material, but also because of the distinction in their use. As we have seen, fillets were worn by both the sacrificer and the victim (as well as by the victorious athlete). But the crown of vegetation, the mark of the sacrificer and the victorious athlete, was not worn by the victim. If the crown were simply, like the fillets, a mark of consecration, one would expect it to be placed upon the head of the consecrated victim. But there is no evidence that this was done by the Greeks. Frazer, on the other hand, ignores the shape of the crown and emphasizes its material. For him the crown is an element of vegetation magic, and served to designate the human representative of the "tree-spirit or the spirit of vegetation." [32] This is perhaps more satisfactory. The victorious athlete was not only crowned with vegetation, but was also given a branch of palm or of some other kind of tree to hold (Figs. 1–4, 6). It may thus be possible to connect the Greek athlete with Frazer's May Kings and Leaf Men. And, inasmuch as Greek athletic festivals often have connections with vegetation cults, we may be satisfied with this explanation.

With the clear-sightedness that is characteristic of genius, however, my wife has pointed out to me what is undoubtedly the true origin of the crown of vegetation. It is nothing other than an element of the primitive hunter's camouflage. This explains why it was worn by the sacrificing priest but not by the victim. (We have seen that the victorious athlete adopts the rôles of both victim and sacrificer, so the crown is appropriate to him.) This also explains the nature of the vegetation of which these crowns were made. For crowns were not normally made from cultivated plants—which is what one would expect if they functioned as "vegetation magic"—but from wild plants. Thus the worshippers of Dionysus did not wreathe themselves with the vine, the cultivation of which was owed to that god, but with ivy. We read in Plutarch that this practice was explained also as an invention of Dionysus, who taught his followers, to the delight of structuralists, to crown themselves with the psychrophyte ivy as an antidote to the inflammatory properties of the vine. [33] Likewise victors at the Olympic Games were not crowned with leaves from a cultivated olive tree (*elaia*), but from the wild olive (*kotinos*), the fruit of which is inedible. [34] And the victors at the other Panhellenic Games were given prizes consisting only of crowns of vegetation (for which reason these four festivals were known

32. Frazer, *Magic Art* II 79–87.
33. Plutarch, *Table Talk* 3.1.3 (= *Moralia* 647a).
34. L. Drees, *Olympia: Gods, Artists, and Athletes,* English translation (New York, 1968) 35.

as "crown contests"). At the Isthmian Games the prize was (apparently at different times) either a crown of pine or a crown of wild celery.[35] The latter was also the prize given at the Nemean Games. At the Pythian Games the prize was a wreath of laurel, the tree sacred to Apollo, in whose honor the games were held. (In addition to athletic contests, there were also musical competitions at the Pythian Games, for which reason the practice was revived in the Renaissance of crowning poets with laurel. England still has a poet laureate and the New York Philharmonic a conductor laureate.)

The original purpose of crowning the head with these forms of vegetation was not to encourage the growth of inedible berries and useless vines. Rather it was to enable the hunter to get close enough to his prey to assure him of at least a fair opportunity to hit it. For the weapons of the primitive hunter are of limited range and accuracy, and he must depend upon his knowledge of the habits of his quarry and upon his skill in approaching without alarming it. Needless to say, the hunter must avoid making any noise that would call the animal's attention to his presence. This precaution survived in the ritual silence prescribed during sacrifice and rationalized by both the Greeks and modern commentators as a safeguard against uttering any word of ill omen. Clearly, however, the pragmatic concerns of the primitive hunter were the origin of such silence. Likewise the hunter attempts to deceive his prey by masking his own scent and by disguising his appearance. He masks his scent, as we have seen above, by bathing frequently before the hunt or by fumigating himself. He may also rub a variety of substances on his body for the same purpose. He disguises himself in many instances by wearing the skins or horns of his prey, a practice attested in wall paintings from prehistoric times. Or he may disguise himself by wearing or carrying various forms of vegetation to blend in with his surroundings. Thus, whatever tree or bush is most common in the hunting area is what is adopted for disguise. This accounts for the great variety of trees, shrubs and vines used by the Greeks in making crowns for priests and victorious athletes. In the course of time, particular plants were associated with particular divinities and locations. So the wild olive was considered to be sacred to Zeus, the laurel to Apollo, ivy to Dionysus. The use of vegetation for disguise accounts, moreover, for the fact that victorious athletes were also given branches of palm or other vegetation to

---

35. Plutarch, *Table Talk* 5.3 (= *Moralia* 675d–677b); cf. O. Broneer, "The Isthmian Victory Crown," *American Journal of Archaeology* 66 (1962) 259–63.

hold (Figs. 1–4, 6), from which we can infer that it was not the shape of the crown that was significant, but the vegetation itself.

Nor is evidence lacking that hunters use precisely these methods of disguise. The Bushman of South Africa, for example, "would stalk his quarry using what natural cover was available, but where this was absent, he would resort to carrying small bushes or wearing a fillet of grass on his head."[36] This practice is particularly common among the aborigines of Australia (Figs. 5, 7, 9). For noosing waterfowl "the native binds a quantity of grass or weeds around his head, and then . . . plunges into the water."[37] The hunters of New South Wales "would sometimes stalk kangaroos, holding in front of them boughs of trees or bushy young saplings."[38] The turkey bustard is caught by a hunter holding a noose who "gradually creeps forward unobserved, enveloped in boughs and bushes."[39] The emu hunter "rubs himself with earth to get rid of any smell from the body; then with bushes in front of him and a collar-like head-dress in some parts, he makes for the bird."[40] The hunters of the Tattayarra tribe "are peculiarly expert in spearing the emu and the kangaroo. This they accomplish by sneaking behind a screen made of bushes tied together, which they carry in one hand."[41] Nor is this technique unknown among the American Indians. The Sioux, for example, "trapped for crows and magpie . . . by concealing themselves in clumps of small pines and covering themselves with pine bows [sic]."[42] Like so many other features of primitive hunting practice, the use of camouflage continued in vestigial form after hunting ceased to be the primary means of providing food. Greek hunters of the historical period are not known to have used such camouflage; the evidence we have concerns sportsmen, for whom disguises were presumably "unsportsmanlike." But the priest wreathed his head before slaughtering the sacrificial beast. And the victorious athlete wore a crown of vegeta-

36. P. Vinnicombe, *People of the Eland* (Pietermaritzburg, 1976) 288.

37. E. J. Eyre, *Journals of Expeditions of Discovery into Central Australia* II (London, 1845) 285; cf. W. E. Roth, *Ethnological Studies among the North-West-Central Queensland Aborigines* (Brisbane, 1897) 99.

38. K. L. Parker, *The Euahlayi Tribe* (London, 1905) 107; cf. R. B. Smyth, *The Aborigines of Victoria* II (London, 1878) 297, and especially J. G. Wood, *The Natural History of Man* II (London, 1870) 44–46.

39. Roth, *Ethnological Studies* 98.

40. N. W. Thomas, *Natives of Australia* (London, 1906) 100; cf. E. Delessert, *Voyages dans les deux océans, Atlantique et Pacifique 1844 à 1847* I (Paris, 1848) 137–38.

41. G. F. Angas, *Savage Life and Scenes in Australia and New Zealand* I (London, 1847) 73.

42. R. B. Hassrick, *The Sioux: Life and Customs of a Warrior Society* (Norman, Okla., 1964) 196.

tion and held branches in his hands as a token of his sacrificial character. Thus, from a pragmatic measure designed to secure success in the hunt, crowns and branches became symbols of success.

Victors in all athletic competitions in ancient Greece were given these crowns and branches as tokens of victory. The unique character-istic of the four Crown, or Panhellenic, Games (the Olympic, Pythian, Isthmian and Nemean Games) was that these were the only prizes awarded by the officials. But at all other athletic festivals more substan-tial prizes were given in addition to the symbolic prizes of vegetation. The prize most frequently mentioned in the literary sources and most commonly depicted in artistic representations is a kind of bronze caul-dron called a *lebēs,* often supported by a tripod. Frequently this combi-nation of *lebēs* and tripod (which was itself commonly referred to simply as a tripod) was given as a prize. Thus, when Achilles sets out the prizes for the contests at the funeral games for Patroclus, the first items Homer mentions are "cauldrons [*lebētes*] and tripods."[43] The first (and appar-ently most important) contest to be held is the chariot race, and the prizes for the winner are a woman and "a tripod with handles, having a capacity of twenty-two measures."[44] Now, the fact that the capacity of the tripod is indicated shows that the prize is in fact not merely a tripod, in the sense of a three-legged support, but a tripod plus cauldron, that is to say, a three-legged *lebēs.* Similarly, the prize for the winner of the wrestling match is "a large tripod that stands over the fire."[45] Again, this is a three-legged cooking vessel, a valuable cauldron worth three times as much as the woman who serves as the prize for the loser of the match. (The match is eventually declared a tie, and Achilles instructs the competitors to take the prizes in equal measure. One wonders how the division was effected in the case of the woman.) When Achilles pursues Hector in front of the city of Troy, Homer compares the activity to the situation when "about the turnposts racing single-foot horses run at full speed, when a great prize is laid up for their winning, a tripod or a woman."[46] Likewise, in his First Isthmian Ode, Pindar sings of the legendary heroes Castor and Iolaus who, as a result of their success in the games, "decorated their homes with tripods and cauldrons [*lebētes-sin*] and golden chalices."[47] A bronze cauldron given as a prize can be seen in the British Museum (Fig. 13). It dates from the sixth century

43. *Iliad* 23.259.
44. *Iliad* 23.264.
45. *Iliad* 23.702.
46. *Iliad* 22.162–64; cf. 11.700. Trans. R. Lattimore (Chicago, 1951).
47. Pindar, *Isthmian Odes* 1.19–20.

B.C. and bears an inscription that reads, "I was set out as a prize at the games of Onomastus, son of Pheidilaus." And vessels of just this shape are depicted next to a pair of wrestlers on an Etruscan tomb painting (much influenced by Greek art) from the fifth century B.C. (Fig. 14). Cauldrons and tripods are frequently shown on vase paintings and other works of art in connection with scenes of athletics and sport.[48] On a coin from the island of Cos, a tripod is shown just behind an athlete who is throwing the discus (Fig. 12). On the François Vase, painted about 575 B.C., the chariot race at the funeral of Patroclus is shown, and in the background is the tripod that serves as prize (Fig. 15). On a black-figure ceramic fragment from the sixth century B.C., we see a pair of boxers contending for a prize tripod (Fig. 16).

Now, what is the significance of these tripods? They are frequently found as dedicatory offerings at Olympia and at the sites of other athletic festivals. M. I. Finley and H. W. Pleket explain that "eventually they became the conventional symbol on painted vases for Games prizes, presumably because of the references to tripods and cauldrons as 'treasure' in the Homeric poems."[49] It is true that tripods and cauldrons are commonly mentioned by Homer as gifts and heirlooms,[50] but this is not an adequate explanation. For we are not told why the Greeks considered these objects "treasures" or "heirlooms." Indeed, if we can find a specific connection between these objects and athletics, it may be more attractive to explain their status as treasures and heirlooms in terms of the fact that they were offered as prizes in the games. If we recognize athletics as a form of sacrificial ritual, such a connection is not far to seek. For the primary function of the *lebēs* was to serve as the vessel in which sacrificial meat was boiled. Herodotus tells us of a miracle that occurred when Hippocrates, the father of the Athenian tyrant Peisistratus, attended the Olympic Games: "After he had slaughtered the sacrificial animals, the cauldrons [*lebētes*], standing ready filled with meat and water, boiled over without the benefit of fire."[51] Herodotus also says that, since the Egyptians revere cows above all other animals, "no Egyptian man or woman would kiss a Greek man on the mouth, or use a Greek's knife, spit or cauldron [*lebēti*]."[52] That is, the *lebēs* of a Greek would certainly be polluted, from the Egyptian point

48. T. B. L. Webster, *Potter and Patron in Classical Athens* (London, 1972) 152–54.
49. M. I. Finley and H. W. Pleket, *The Olympic Games: The First Thousand Years* (London, 1976) pl. 7(c).
50. *Iliad* 9.123, 24.233; *Odyssey* 13.13, 15.84, 17.222.
51. Herodotus, *Histories* 1.59.1.
52. Herodotus, *Histories* 2.41.3.

of view, because its normal function was to serve as the vessel in which oxen, both male and female, were cooked after they had been sacrificed. Since the purpose of sacrifice is to ensure the continuation of life through destruction, a number of myths arose according to which re-vivification or rejuvenation takes place as a result of dismemberment and subsequent boiling in a *lebēs*. Medea rejuvenated an old ram by this method, and persuaded the daughters of her enemy Pelias to attempt the same procedure on their father.[53] (It did not work.) There is an Orphic account of how the Titans dismembered the god Dionysus and boiled his limbs in a *lebēs*. It is generally recognized that this myth represents ritual rebirth.[54] The same is the case with the myth of Tantalus. When he entertained the gods at a feast, he could think of nothing more appropriate to serve them than his own son. So he chopped up his son Pelops, put the pieces in a *lebēs*, boiled them and served them to the gods. The gods, of course, were outraged at this impiety, and Zeus ordered Hermes to put the meat back into the cauldron and thus to restore Pelops to life.[55] The particular significance of this last myth is that it was precisely Pelops who was considered to be the founder of the Olympic Games.[56] The tomb and shrine of Pelops were located within the Altis, the sacred precinct of Zeus at Olympia. And the great Temple of Zeus in the Altis was surmounted by a *lebēs*, the symbol, as it were, of Pelops' fate. And there is perhaps evidence that this was originally the prize offered to the victors at Olympia, as is known to have been the case elsewhere. For, when Nestor tells the story of his youthful adventures, he mentions that a great debt was owed to his father Neleus "in shining Elis," the territory of Olympia. The debt consisted, in Lattimore's translation, of "four horses, race-competitors with their own chariot, who were on their way to a race and were to run for a tripod."[57]

If sport is indeed a form of ritual sacrifice, it is entirely appropriate that a sacrificial vessel was the most common form of prize in ancient Greece. And it is tempting to believe that these vessels were the originals of the symbolic prizes frequently awarded even today in athletic

53. Diodorus of Sicily, *The Library of History* 4.52; Ovid, *Metamorphoses* 7.297–349.
54. Guépin, *Tragic Paradox* 244; cf., however, M. Detienne, *Dionysos Slain*, English translation (Baltimore, 1979) 68–94.
55. The ancient commentaries (scholia) to Pindar, *Olympian Odes* 1.40.
56. Burkert, *Homo Necans* 93–103.
57. *Iliad* 11.699–700. Also, large bronze tripods were a common form of dedicatory offering at Olympia from at least as early as the eighth century B.C. (F. Willemsen, *Drei-fusskessel von Olympia*, Olympische Forschungen 3 [Berlin, 1957]).

competitions. As far as I am aware, no one has troubled himself over the question of why plates, cups and other apparatus of the dining table should be given out as tokens of supremacy in sport. (Indeed, I am not aware of the existence of any serious study of the history of prizes in sport, a subject that would well reward scholarly attention.) But the trophy for ice hockey in North America is the Stanley Cup. Lawn tennis has its Davis Cup and Wightman Cup, and the prize given at Wimbledon is also a cup. Since 1922 there has been the Walker Cup in golf, since 1927 the Ryder Cup and, since 1932, the Curtis Cup. The World Cup is the prize for association football, and the Thomas Cup the prize for badminton. But the practice of awarding cups has an even longer connection with the sport of yachting. The prize now known as the *America's* Cup was first awarded in 1851, but similar prizes had been associated with the sport for some time before that. I have been unable to trace the practice beyond 13 July 1775, on which date a race was held for the prize of a silver cup offered by Henry Frederick, duke of Cumberland. This gentleman, of whom the *Dictionary of National Biography* in characteristically understated fashion records that he was "coarse and brutal in his everyday life" and "notorious for excesses," drank a libation from the prize cup before presenting it to the owner of the victorious *Aurora,* a Mr. Parkes. The duke continued the practice of offering (and, apparently, emptying) cups for some years. The last of the Cumberland cups was won in 1782 by the owner of the *Caroline,* and found its way in the following century to a pawnshop in San Francisco.[58] It is not possible to determine what the duke's motive in offering such a prize was, apart perhaps from his evident fondness for vessels of various sorts. There are, however, isolated pieces of evidence for cups as prizes in other sports before the time of the duke of Cumberland. Although the prize for which competitors in the famous horse races at Siena ran was a piece of cloth, there is mention also of a silver goblet as a subsidiary prize as early as the beginning of the eighteenth century.[59] Cups are attested as prizes for horseraces even earlier in Lincolnshire. We learn that in the first half of the seventeenth century there were races every Thursday in March in the town of Stamford, the prize for which was "a silver and gilt Cup with a cover, to the value of seaven or eight pounds, provided by the care of the Alderman."[60] And on Thursday, 3 April

58. A. H. Clark, *The History of Yachting 1600–1815* (New York, 1904) 197–202.
59. W. Heywood, *Palio and Ponte* (London, 1904) 221.
60. R. Butcher, *The Survey and Antiquitie of the Towne of Stamford in the County of Lincolne* (London, 1646) 39.

1617, James I witnessed a race run for a cup on the heath at Lincoln.[61] Earlier still, a "Cupp of Golde, woorth LX marcs" is mentioned as a prize in a mediaeval tournament.[62] Unfortunately, the nature of the evidence makes it impossible to determine whether there is a direct link between ancient and modern practice, although the historical association of sport and sacramental meal encourages us to seek such a link.

A waggish graduate student once proffered the Holy Grail as a solution to this dilemma, and, although the suggestion was made in jest, I would not dismiss it out of hand. After all, the Holy Grail is a more suitable archetype than the duke of Cumberland's cup. An examination of the origins and influence of the legend of the Grail is beyond the competence of the present writer and, in any case, it is of perhaps limited relevance in an essay on the nature of Greek sport. Nevertheless, the coincidences between the Grail and athletic prizes are striking enough that, even if a direct line of descent cannot be proven, it is worth while to sketch them briefly here in hopes that this will provide a stimulus to further research. To begin with, the Grail is associated with a sacramental meal, indeed the archetypical sacramental meal for Christians, the Last Supper. And it is involved with blood sacrifice, inasmuch as the blood of Christ is supposed to have been gathered in the Grail. Furthermore, the legend of the Grail is connected with death and rebirth in two ways: in the first place, it is a relic of the death and resurrection of Christ; in the second place, it is the instrument whereby the ailing king is cured and, in some versions, rejuvenated. The Grail is the object of a quest, and can be won only by attaining success in tests and contests. Galahad, like the successful athlete, must observe strict sexual continence. There is, of course, a difficulty, and it is one that is justifiably emphasized in Jessie L. Weston's book *From Ritual to Romance* (which, by coincidence, immediately follows Guttmann's *From Ritual to Record* in the card catalogue), namely that the Grail is a drinking vessel, not a cauldron.[63] And indeed, according to the most likely etymology, the word *grail* derives ultimately from the Greek word *krater*, which designates a vessel in which wine was mixed with water.[64] But the interesting feature of this etymology is that, while it appears to reinforce the idea

61. J. Nichols, *The Progresses, Processions, and Magnificent Festivities, of King James the First* III (London, 1828) 265.

62. F. H. Cripps-Day, *The History of the Tournament in England and in France* (London, 1918) xxxviii.

63. J. L. Weston, *From Ritual to Romance* (Cambridge, 1920) 69–70.

64. H. and R. Kahane, "Wolframs Gral und Wolframs Kyot," *Zeitschrift für deutsches Altertum* 89 (1959) 191–200.

of the Grail as drinking vessel, in reality it does no such thing. For a krater is not in fact a drinking vessel, but a large bowl from which wine is drawn into smaller vessels for drinking. A krater is often as large as a *lebēs* and, like a *lebēs,* is sometimes supported by a tripod. And there are some interesting associations between the krater and the *lebēs,* facilitated, I would assume, by the myth alluded to above concerning the dismemberment of Dionysus. For Dionysus, as the embodiment of wine, ought to reside in a krater, but he is in the myth boiled in a *lebēs.* The significance of the myth is clearly that blood sacrifice is necessary for the fecundity of the vegetation just as, in the Grail legend, the vessel containing the blood of Christ is necessary for the restoration of fruitfulness to the Waste Land.[65] And the krater, like the *lebēs,* has associations with the notion of death and resurrection. At the end of the fourth century B.C. the remains of a wealthy Macedonian were buried in a spectacular gilt bronze krater decorated with Dionysiac motifs. The presence of this vessel in a funerary context, as well as the existence of a large number of ceramic kraters, especially from southern Italy, that are elaborately painted with scenes depicting the underworld indicate the connection between the krater and the various mystery cults that began to be popular in the fourth century B.C. and that held out to their worshippers hopes for a blessed afterlife.

Associations between krater and *lebēs* were already being made by the end of the second century after Christ, if we may judge from a confused and curious, but nonetheless enlightening, passage in Athenaeus, a Greek writer who lived in Rome at that time. Here is C. B. Gulick's translation, which I shall interrupt for comment:

> Philochorus says that drinkers not only reveal what they are, but also disclose the secrets of everybody else in their outspokenness. Hence the saying, "wine is truth also," and "wine revealeth the heart of man."

Philochorus was an Athenian who wrote about 300 B.C. Unfortunately, it is impossible to tell how much of what follows is to be attributed to him. Athenaeus continues:

---

65. See Guépin, *Tragic Paradox;* Burkert, *Homo Necans* 44–45; A. B. Cook, *Zeus: A Study in Ancient Religion* II (Cambridge, 1925) 210–21. For other associations between Dionysus and Christ, see R. Eisler, *Orphisch-Dionysische Mysteriengedanken in der christlichen Antike,* Vorträge der Bibliothek Warburg 2.2 (1922–23) 235–48; O. Weinreich, "Gebet und Wunder: Zwei Abhandlungen zur Religions- und Literaturgeschichte," in *Genethliakon Wilhelm Schmid,* Tübinger Beiträge zur Altertumswissenschaft 5 (1929) 336–41.

> Hence also the tripod as prize of victory in the festival of Dionysus.

This refers not, it is true, to an athletic contest, but to the Athenian contest in the performance of the dithyramb, a cult song in honor of Dionysus.[66]

> For of those who speak the truth we say that they "speak from the tripod," and it must be understood that the mixing-bowl [*krater*] is Dionysus's tripod.

The proverbial expression "to speak from the tripod" in fact referred to the veracity of the priestess of Apollo at Delphi, who spoke while seated upon a tripod. It is difficult to say whether Athenaeus is being quite serious here when he associates this proverb with the proverbial *in vino veritas*. What is of significance to us, however, is that Athenaeus is going out of his way to associate krater and *lebēs*. This becomes clearer in the sequel:

> For in ancient times there were two sorts of tripods, both of which came to be called cauldrons [*lebētes*]. The one called "bath-pourer" was also made to stand over a fire. . . . The other is the so-called *krater* ("mixing-bowl"). Homer: "seven tripods, unspoiled by fire." In these they used to mix their wine, and this is "the veritable tripod of truth." Wherefore the tripod is proper to Apollo because of its prophetic truth, while to Dionysus it is proper because of the truth of wine.[67]

This confusion between krater and *lebēs* can explain why the Grail is associated with rebirth and rejuvenation. Just as the *lebēs* was used by Medea to confer renewed youth, so the Grail, according to Wolfram von Eschenbach, bestows eternal youth. And we can also explain in this way why the Grail is regarded as a trophy. In their fascinating study of the Hermetic sources of the Grail legend, Henry and Renée Kahane show that Wolfram's conception of the Grail as a prize to be won derives from a passage in the Hermetic Corpus according to which God willed that wisdom or intellect (*nous,* the same word that was translated "heart" above, in the proverbial saying quoted by Athenaeus, "wine revealeth the heart of man") be established as a prize for men to win.[68]

---

66. A. Pickard-Cambridge, *The Dramatic Festivals of Athens,* second edition (Oxford, 1968) 77–78.

67. Athenaeus, *The Deipnosophists* 37e–f, trans. C. B. Gulick (London, 1927).

68. H. and R. Kahane, *The Krater and the Grail: Hermetic Sources of the Parzival,* Illinois Studies in Language and Literature 56 (Urbana, Ill., 1965) 66–67.

The word *prize* is, in the Greek, *athlon,* the word that normally refers to prizes in athletic contests and that is, indeed, the origin of the English word "athletics." And the form of this prize is a krater that God has filled with *nous.* In addition, God appoints a herald to make a proclamation concerning the prize, a herald who is surely intended to recall those who played so important a rôle at the Olympic Games and at the other athletic contests.[69]

But this is a path of speculation upon which angels would surely fear to embark, and even the purest of fools might hesitate before rushing in. We must leave Günter Grass' Athlete on the Cross and return to the facts of Greek sport as we know them. One of the most curious features of Greek athletics, and one about which we have a considerable amount of evidence, is the extensive use made by Greek athletes of olive oil. It was the regular practice of Greek athletes to rub olive oil over their bodies before exercise or competition, and to scrape the oil off with a curved metal implement, called a strigil, after exercise. Containers of olive oil and strigils are among the objects most commonly depicted on vase paintings in connection with athletics, and we have already referred to Lysippus' famous statue representing an athlete scraping himself off with a strigil. On a red-figure vase in Berkeley (Fig. 25), we see a young man coming from his music lesson and his athletic trainer holding out a strigil to him, as if to say, "Put down that lyre and get ready for some serious physical exercise!" Here the strigil is simply a symbol for exercise, for the young man will not need it until after his workout. Likewise, anointing the body with olive oil is so closely associated with sport that it too is used as a symbol for sport. Inscriptions, for example, sometimes use the expression "the anointed ones" to mean "young men engaged in physical training."[70] And it is clear from the literary sources that anointing with olive oil before exercise and scraping the oil off afterwards had become a fixed ritual among Greek athletes.

What was the origin and purpose of this practice? The evidence that we have for the ancient Greeks' view of the matter comes, unfortunately, from a source that is difficult to assess, namely, a satirical dialogue entitled *Anacharsis* by Lucian, who lived in the second century after Christ. The work consists of a fictional conversation between the Athenian poet and lawgiver Solon and the foreigner Anacharsis. The

69. *Corpus Hermeticum* 4.4. Heralds were of such importance at the Olympic Games that separate competitions for heralds were instituted at the Games in 396 B.C.

70. E.g., W. Dittenberger, *Orientis Graeci inscriptiones selectae* I (Leipzig, 1903) 542, no. 339.72, and II (Leipzig, 1905) 510, no. 764.5.

latter is puzzled by the athletic practices of the Greeks and asks Solon to explain the meaning of what are, to Anacharsis, bizarre and outlandish customs. Inasmuch as Lucian's purpose is satirical, we must contend with the possibility, even likelihood, that Solon's explanations are intended to appear as absurd to Lucian's readers as Greek athletics appear to Anacharsis. At any rate, the explanation that Solon gives of the practice of anointing with olive oil gives the impression of being quite reasonable. In section 24 of the dialogue, Solon indicates that, just as one rubs leather with olive oil to make it more elastic, so athletes use olive oil to make their limbs more supple.[71] Whether Lucian intended this as a serious explanation, and whether Greek athletes themselves believed that this was the reason they anointed themselves, we have no means of determining with certainty. But it cannot be entirely correct. If it were, we would expect the Greeks to have anointed themselves with olive oil constantly, and not only immediately before exercise. In section 28 of the dialogue, Solon seems to hint at a different (and incompatible) explanation. In response to Anacharsis' query about wrestlers rolling about in the mud as they grapple with one another, Solon replies that this practice provides good training for young men and has useful military applications. For the mud, along with the sweat and the olive oil, serves to make the wrestlers more slippery, and the practice that the young men get makes them more capable of carrying wounded comrades off the battlefield and of capturing enemy soldiers. But neither can this be a correct explanation. In the first place, it does not explain why boxers, runners and other athletes anointed themselves.[72] In the second place, it ignores the fact that wrestlers dusted themselves with sand or powder, thus counteracting the slipperiness that the olive oil imparted.[73] But we have learned that, when dealing with ritual activities, it is frequently the case that those who engage in those activities cannot be relied on to give an adequate explanation of their behavior. It is likely that the Greeks had no idea why they anointed themselves with olive oil before they exercised.

71. Compare Livy 21.55.1. One is reminded of Father William, who says, in Alice's version:

> I kept all my limbs very supple
> By the use of this ointment—one shilling the box—
> Allow me to sell you a couple?

72. See, for example, Quintus Curtius Rufus 9.7.16–20; Callimachus, *Hymns* 5.25; Ovid, *Metamorphoses* 10.176.
73. Harris, *Greek Athletes* 103.

Christoph Ulf calls into question the various attempts that have been made to explain this Greek practice in rational terms.[74] According to Ulf, the Greeks used olive oil because they felt that it had the ability to make them stronger. Since there is no evidence that olive oil in fact has such an ability, Ulf ascribes the practice to the "magico-religious" sphere. That olive oil was considered by the Greeks (and by other peoples) to have "magical" properties is beyond doubt, and Ulf correctly notes the Greek practice of anointing statues of the gods, grave stelae and other objects with oil. He also points out the evidence that the Greeks believed in the curative power of olive oil. Ulf is certainly correct in asserting that Greek athletes anointed themselves because they felt that the oil possessed some property that would enhance their athletic performance, but he is also guilty of a certain vagueness of argumentation that we are now in a position to clarify. It is very comforting to explain something in terms of "magic" or "religion" because, these being non-rational phenomena and having, at the same time, a certain universal application, they can conveniently be used to "explain" other troublesome non-rational phenomena. But it takes only a moment's reflection to recognize that this is a fraudulent procedure. If we have two unexplained phenomena, what justifies us in explaining the first in terms of the second rather than the second in terms of the first? Ulf seems to assume that magic and religion (which he appears to yoke in dubious identity) are givens, and that they are already securely explained. Anything that is magical or religious (like anointing with olive oil) is available for use to explain something else. The Greeks used olive oil to anoint the statues of the gods. Therefore olive oil has magical powers. Therefore it can be used to increase the strength of athletes. The inadequacy of this line of reasoning is fairly evident. Either the Greeks anointed statues of the gods with olive oil because they believed that the oil possessed magical powers, in which case we are entitled to inquire into the origins of the belief in these magical powers, or the Greeks believed that olive oil possessed magical powers because of its association with the practice of anointing statues, in which case we are entitled to inquire into the origins of this practice. Only if we believe that olive oil in fact possesses magical powers or if we believe in the existence of supernatural entities that make arbitrary demands on their worshippers is the explanation in terms of "magic" or "religion" ade-

74. Christoph Ulf, "Die Einreibung der griechischen Athleten mit Öl," *Stadion* 5 (1979) 220–38.

quate. Otherwise we are entitled to expect a rational explanation either for the practice of anointing statues of the gods or for the belief in magical properties of olive oil.

As it happens, we can give a rational explanation for the belief in magical properties of olive oil. In other words, the truth is just the opposite of what Ulf supposes. The religious associations of olive oil do not "explain" the practice of Greek athletes; rather the practice of rubbing oil (and other substances) on the body is a very ancient one and itself explains the belief in magical properties. We have seen that it is possible to account for a number of the elements of sacrificial ritual as survivals from the time of the primitive hunter. We can account for this practice in the same way. One means of enhancing chances for success on the hunt is for the hunter to ensure that he get as close as possible to his prey without alerting the animal to his presence. The hunter does this by various means of disguise and camouflage. He may disguise himself as an animal: the Eskimo wears a sealskin when hunting seals, the Plains Indian wears a buffalo hide or antlers, the Indian of the forest uses a moose-call to imitate the sound of his prey. Or, as we have seen above, he may conceal himself behind a screen or under a wreath of vegetation. These disguises are intended to prevent the quarry from seeing the hunter. But the hunter is well aware that the animal (like the hunter himself) does not rely solely upon visual clues. The hunter must, if he is to be successful, also prevent his prey from hearing him and from smelling him. While stalking, he maintains a silence that is the origin of the awed silence of sacrifice and of the church. And he uses various means to conceal his own scent. He can do this in either of two ways. Either he can minimize his body odor by "purifying" himself or by inhibiting perspiration. Or he can mask his odor by applying various substances to the body.

The elephant hunters among the Pygmies, for example, use a particularly effective method of masking their scent. "If they happen upon some fresh elephant-dung, they smear themselves with it in order to conceal the scent of their own body."[75] When hunting for eagles a Cheyenne "greased his whole body with eagle fat so as to conceal the human scent."[76] An Apache informant recommends that, "When you are going hunting you take care not to clean yourself up. Perhaps you

---

75. P. Schebesta, *Die Bambuti-Pygmäen vom Ituri* II.1 (Brussels, 1941) 109.
76. G. B. Grinnell, *The Cheyenne Indians: Their History and Ways of Life* I (New Haven, Conn., 1923) 302–3.

have been eating the meat of some animal and therefore have been rubbing the grease and marrow of the long bones on your face, legs, and
arms. You keep this on." Also, you should not chew onions or even dig
them up before hunting, for "the deer will smell you if you do."[77] According to the fifth-century Greek writer Hecataeus, the barbarian
Paeones were in the habit of anointing themselves with butter.[78] A procedure particularly favored by aboriginal hunters of Australia is the use
of mud for smearing on the body. "In the Cloncurry District the Mita-
koodi's commonest plan of catching emus is to sneak up to them while
feeding and spear them. . . . To prevent the bird 'smelling' him, he gets
rid of the perspiration from under the armpits and from between the
thighs by rubbing these parts with earth."[79] (It is to be noted that sumo
wrestlers frequently wipe their armpits to remove the perspiration before a match.) The use of mud for this purpose is known also among
North American hunters. "Apache hunting techniques observed in the
1500s and early 1600s were covert rather than overt. Then, as later, the
Apaches seem to have been masters of camouflage, hiding behind brush
shelters at watering places or lying, covered with local mud, in the buffalo trails."[80] This is a particularly useful practice, as it serves a double
purpose. The mud not only masks the hunter's odor, but also makes
him more difficult to see, as he blends into the surroundings. Thus,
among Australian aborigines, for example: "In the usual method of
hunting kangaroos, a man or several men cover themselves with mud to
prevent the kangaroo from seeing and smelling them."[81]

The evidence presented above shows that the need for the hunter to
conceal his scent from his prey is widely recognized, and that hunters
from Africa, Australia and North America are well acquainted with effective methods of doing so. The original reason for these practices
begins to be lost sight of as hunting begins to lose its importance as a
society's primary means of securing food and as technological advances
(bow and arrow, domestication of the horse and so on) make it less

77. M. E. Opler, *An Apache Life-Way* (Chicago, 1941) 316.
78. Athenaeus, *The Deipnosophists* 447d.
79. Roth, *Ethnological Studies* (cited n. 37, p. 87, above) 97–98; cf. E. Eylmann,
Die Eingeborenen der Kolonie Südaustralien (Berlin, 1908) 272. The quotation marks
around "smelling" are justified by the fact that birds in general do not have a keen sense of
smell. But can the aborigine learn this without exposing himself to the risk of starvation?
80. D. A. Gunnerson, *The Jicarilla Apaches: A Study in Survival* (De Kalb, Ill., 1974)
143.
81. W. L. Warner, *A Black Civilization,* revised edition (New York, 1958) 140; cf.
B. Anell, *Hunting and Trapping Methods in Australia and Oceania,* Studia Ethnographica
Upsaliensia 18 (Uppsala, 1960) 15–16.

essential for the hunter to get close to the animal without being noticed. But humans are so tenacious of their patterns of behavior that these practices, which were once essential for success, became ritualized as "magic" and "religion." We can see the border between pragmatic act and magic in the process of being crossed in an account of the practices of an African tribe, the Krobo, which is basically an agricultural society that engages in occasional hunting.[82] A member of this tribe seeks out a medicine-man before he goes hunting in order to secure "medicine." The hunter is given some seeds, which he puts into his mouth and then spits out onto some leaves. These leaves are then added to water, and the resulting brew is given to the hunter to drink and to wash in. Other leaves are crushed and roasted, producing a black powder that is rubbed into cuts made "on all important parts of the hunter's body." It is clear that the tribe retains some vague notion of the original function of this practice, for the medicine is believed by the hunter "to help him to get close to the animals without being noticed." But the reason the medicine possesses this efficacy, namely the fact that it disguises the hunter's scent, is no longer known. The medicine is now felt to have magical properties, for it is also believed "to protect the hunter from his possible enemies." That it is now a magical substance is also indicated by the way in which it is used. Not only is it applied to the body, but it is also ingested, presumably in order to impart its potency to the hunter more directly. And this, surely, is also the reason for the rubbing of the powder into incisions in the "important parts" of the body. The same practice is observed by the Cherokee ball players before a game. After they have undergone the ordeal of scratching, "the shaman then gives to each player a small piece of root. . . . The men chew these roots and spit out the juice over their limbs and bodies, rubbing it well into the scratches."[83] That the original reason for rubbing the roots over the body was to mask the human scent is shown, for example, by the practice of the Paiute Indians of California. Among these Indians, "siupa (*Distichlis Spicata* Greene), salt grass gum was chewed and put on hands and feet when setting traps to deodorize them."[84]

These observations enable us to understand a curious piece of medical lore preserved in the copious writings of the Roman polymath Pliny

82. H. Huber, *The Krobo: Traditional Social and Religious Life of a West African People* (St. Augustin near Bonn, 1963) 282–83.

83. Mooney, "Cherokee Ball-Play" 122 (= Culin, *Games of the North American Indians* 581).

84. J. H. Steward, "Ethnography of the Owens Valley Paiute," *University of California Publications in American Archaeology and Ethnography* 33 (1933) 254 n. 53.

the Elder, who was killed by the eruption of Vesuvius in A.D. 79. According to Pliny, it was thought that the application of the dung of wild boars was an efficacious treatment for wounds and ruptures. Its virtues were particularly appreciated by Roman charioteers, who used it as a remedy for the frequent scrapes, wounds and bruises that they incurred when they were dragged by their horses in the Circus. Presumably wild-boar dung had originally served the same purpose as the Pygmies' elephant dung, and it came to have "magical" properties on account of its proven effectiveness in enhancing the boar-hunter's success. Once the efficacy of the boar's dung was attributed to its magical potency, it no longer needed to be applied to the skin in its fresh, pungent state. Instead, Pliny tells us, it was collected during the spring and dried, although in an emergency it could be used fresh as well. Indeed, it no longer needed to be applied to the skin at all. Like the Krobo "medicine," it could be ingested to produce similar benefits. Pliny says:

> There are some who think it more beneficial to boil the dung in vinegar. Moreover, they assure us that this dung, reduced to powder and taken in drink, is curative of ruptures and sprains; for falls from vehicles it should be taken in vinegar. The more recent authorities reduce it to ash and take it in water, saying that even the Emperor Nero used to refresh himself with this draught, since he was ready even by this means to distinguish himself in the three-horse chariot-race. They think that the next most efficacious dung is that of pigs.[85]

What has all of this to do with the practice of the ancient Greeks? According to one authority on ancient sport, "all Greek athletes oiled themselves before exercise as a hygienic measure to keep dirt out of their pores," and it is often asserted that the purpose in using olive oil was to close the pores of the skin.[86] To my knowledge, however, no one has explained why it is of importance to the athlete to close the pores. Indeed, one would think that it would be positively dangerous for an athlete to close the pores and inhibit perspiration, for he would run the risk of overheating. But the hunter in the wild has very good reasons for closing the pores. It is reasonable to assume (although I know of no evidence that olive oil was so used) that at some point olive oil was one of those substances used by primitive European hunters to inhibit perspiration and thus to conceal their scent. As hunting gave way to agri-

---

85. Pliny, *Natural History* 28.238, trans. W. H. S. Jones (Cambridge, Mass., 1963).
86. Harris, *Sport* 21; cf. *Greek Athletes* 102; A. S. Pease in *Paulys Real-Encyclopädie der classischen Altertumswissenschaft* XVII.2 (Stuttgart, 1937) 2462. That olive oil inhibits perspiration is stated explicitly by Celsus (*On Medicine* 3.19.2).

culture, some ten millennia ago, the original purpose of the oil was lost sight of. But, since it had for so long brought success to the hunter, it was felt to possess the ability to improve the hunter's skill, to make him stronger and faster. Since oil was thought to have the power to strengthen, it continued to be used by athletes and others. Man, it seems, would rather rationalize his behavior than alter it. Greek athletes oiled themselves to enhance their performance. The Greek writer Philostratus recommends that athletes receive a massage with olive oil "especially over the upper part of the body"[87]—just as the Krobo hunter rubs his "medicine" into the "important parts" of his body and the Cherokee ball player rubs the magic roots into incisions made in his arms, legs and shoulders. Outside of athletic contexts, it was especially the head that was anointed.[88] The Greek dead were anointed,[89] presumably to restore their strength to them. Such power to confer strength could only come from the gods, and so olive oil became a mark of the divinity. Statues of the gods and altars were anointed, as were kings, the representatives of the gods on earth.[90] Significantly, however, the sacrificial animal, the descendant of the hunter's quarry, was not anointed, despite its consecration to the gods.

With the advent of agriculture there came, in addition to the pall of forgetfulness with regard to the original reason for anointing the body, the cultivation of the olive. The Greeks became conscious of the differing qualities and grades of oil, and even oil fit for consumption was used for anointing. The Greeks oiled themselves not only before exercise but also immediately following the bath, as a regular element of their toilet. It is difficult to account for this habit except as a relic of primitive hunting practice. The hunter would first bathe himself to remove his own body odor, and then he would oil himself to inhibit perspiration. This sequence of activities became ritualized after its original purpose disappeared and, like ritual behavior in general, underwent a certain degree of intensification. The original purpose of bathing and oiling was to neutralize the human scent *so that the hunter would not be noticed* by his prey. When man was no longer a hunter, the apparent purpose, merely to conceal the human scent, could be fulfilled even more effectively. Aromatics were added to the oil. Thus were perfumes born. Aromatics are used not only by the ancient Greeks, of course, but

---

87. See Jüthner, *Philostratos über Gymnastik* 293.
88. Onians, *Origins of European Thought* 210.
89. C. Mayer, *Das Öl im Kultus der Griechen*, diss. (Würzburg, 1917) 25–26.
90. Ibid., passim; Onians, *Origins of European Thought* 188–91.

by civilized men generally. There is, after all, nothing inherently offensive about human body odor. But, because for countless millennia success in securing food depended in part upon the hunter's ability to conceal his odor, a strong body odor became aesthetically unpleasing. The opposite, either the mere absence of odor or even a highly perfumed fragrance, came to be a mark of success. Indeed, among the ancient Greeks a pleasing body odor was regarded as a sign of divinity.[91]

We tend today not to take smell very seriously, and this is perhaps the reason that the observations made above have not previously been made. We have been taught by Freud and his followers that man has had to sacrifice his sense of smell to the development of his cognitive faculties. Today the sense of smell is more or less vestigial, more from desuetude and disinfection than in order to make way for compensatory encroachments from elsewhere. That the capacity still exists is proved by the oenologist, or even the experienced oenophile, who can distinguish a Château Margaux from an Haut-Brion on the basis of bouquet alone. But, outside a very limited area, success no longer depends upon the ability to make fine olfactory discriminations. The hunter whose survival depends on it routinely makes such discriminations, and he assumes (in most cases correctly) that his quarry is equally adept. And so he takes the precautions already mentioned to ensure that the animal does not sense his presence. To these precautions we can add two more, which are often found in conjunction, namely, the fast and the sweat bath. The purpose of the former is revealed by the Apache cited above for the injunction against eating onions before hunting deer. For many foods impart a—for the hunter—dangerous odor to the sweat. This was known, for example, to the fourth-century Greek philosopher Theophrastus, who gives rue as an example of the kind of food that can cause a foul odor in perspiration.[92] The hunter presumably knew, from the evidence provided by his own nose, which foods to avoid, and he acted accordingly. In the course of time, however, as this precaution was ritualized, the intensification characteristic of ritual took effect and the prohibition became more general. If you know that some foods are to be avoided, but are not sure which those foods are, the safest thing to do is to eat nothing at all or, failing that, to restrict your intake to the absolute minimum. Before hunting whales the Indians of Nootka

---

91. E. Lohmeyer, *Vom göttlichen Wohlgeruch,* Sitzungsberichte der Heidelberger Akademie der Wissenschaft 9 (Heidelberg, 1919).

92. Theophrastus, *On Perspiration* 5; cf. "Aristotle," *Problems* 2.13.

Sound fasted for a week, during which time they ate very little. The Tsetsaut Indians of British Columbia fasted for three or four days before hunting. The Hidatsa Indians fasted while hunting eagles. The Arikaras and the "Gros Ventres" ate nothing for four days before going on the warpath.[93]

And, like so many other features of hunting ritual, the fast has been adopted in sacrificial ritual, and in religious ritual generally, as well. Among the ancient Greeks fasting formed part of several religious rituals.[94] (We have already referred to the likelihood that a special diet was imposed upon athletes for a 30-day period before the Olympic Games.) At the Eleusinian Mysteries the sacred meal was preceded by a fast.[95] At the Thesmophoria in Athens the sacrifice in which the festival culminated was preceded by a day devoted to fasting.[96] At another Athenian festival, the Skira, the men fasted while the women feasted. The consumption of large quantities of garlic by the women was characteristic of this feast. This practice is explained by the ancients as designed to make the women unattractive to the men,[97] but it is more likely that its purpose was to emphasize further the contrast between the sexes that this festival celebrated. The women flaunted the fact that they could eat the food that was especially taboo to the hunter, the hunt being "men's work" par excellence. We are also familiar with the fast in connection with sacrificial ritual in religions still current. Among many Christians a natural fast is observed before communion, and Easter is preceded by the forty days of Lent. (According to the widespread folk etymology, "carnival" is literally a farewell to meat.) And the Jewish Day of Atonement is characterized by a fast (following the nearly universal interpretation of the biblical prescription) as well as by a sacrifice of one bullock, one ram, seven yearling lambs and one male goat, plus grain offerings and libations.[98]

Among hunting societies, the sweat bath reinforces the effects of the fast by forcing perspiration and thereby removing from the body the telltale odors of foods previously consumed. The sweat bath was known to the ancient Greeks (in connection with anointing with olive oil and with athletics)[99] and is found among other inhabitants of Eu-

---

93. Frazer, *Taboo* 191, 198–99, 161.
94. P. R. Arbesmann, *Das Fasten bei den Griechen und Römern,* Religionsgeschichtliche Versuche und Vorarbeiten 21 (Giessen, 1929).
95. N. J. Richardson, *The Homeric Hymn to Demeter* (Oxford, 1974) 213.
96. H. W. Parke, *Festivals of the Athenians* (London, 1977) 86–87.
97. Burkert, *Homo Necans* 145.
98. Leviticus 23.27; Numbers 29.7–11.
99. Jüthner, *Philostratos über Gymnastik* 308–10.

rope, but it is particularly common in the Western Hemisphere. Ethnographers record the ritual of the sweat bath among, for example, the Aztecs, the Micmac of Canada, the Apache and the Navaho.[100] That the origin of this ritual is to be found in primitive hunting practice is clear from a number of the features that characterize it. Among the Navaho, for example, the sweat bath is explicitly attested as being used before the hunt,[101] and among the Apache before a race, "to enable them to become good runners." In general the reason the Apache gives for the sweat bath is that it is useful "for good health, for long life, and to cure sickness." The Navaho asserts that the purpose is "to get ugly things out of your body." The Micmac agrees: "The sweat is like slime—so full is it of impurities from one's entire system." But if this is the purpose of the sweat bath, why is it that the Apache women and prepubescent boys are not allowed the benefits of the sweat bath? And why is it mostly men, and only rarely women, among the Micmac and the Navaho who avail themselves of the beneficial effects of the sweat bath? Surely this is because the sweat bath was originally a practice engaged in solely by hunters—that is to say, by men. That it was originally a hunting practice is strongly suggested by other details as well. Among the Micmac "each man has a towel of moose or caribou skin with which he rubs the back of one of his fellows." During the sweat bath the Aztec "switched himself violently with grasses" and the Apache rubbed "pounded piñon needles or pounded juniper" on his body. Similarly, the heated coals and rocks of the Navaho sweat bath were covered with these same plants as well as with various grasses, and the Micmac sweat lodge featured hemlock boughs. Clearly the purpose of all these elements of the sweat bath is to neutralize the human odor and replace it with something that will not alert the bather's animal prey. We have earlier seen animal fats, grasses and other forms of vegetation used for precisely this purpose. In addition, the Navaho sometimes rubs himself

100. J. Soustelle, *The Daily Life of the Aztecs on the Eve of the Spanish Conquest*, English translation (London, 1961) 129–30; W. D. and R. S. Wallis, *The Micmac Indians of Eastern Canada* (Minneapolis, 1955) 123–25; Opler, *Apache Life-Way* (cited n. 77, p. 99, above) 218–20; C. Kluckholm, W. W. Hill, and L. W. Kluckholm, *Navaho Material Culture* (Cambridge, Mass., 1971) 317–27. Also among the Eskimos (K. Birket-Smith, *The Eskimos* [London, 1959] 118), the Kiowa (M. P. Mayhall, *The Kiowas*, second edition [Norman, Okla., 1971] 153–54), the Huron (W. V. Kinietz, *The Indians of the Western Great Lakes 1615–1760* [Ann Arbor, Mich., 1940] 145–46) and various California tribes (R. F. Heizer and M. A. Whipple, eds., *The California Indians: A Source Book* [Berkeley, 1951] 10–11).

101. Also among other tribes: see Heizer and Whipple, eds., *California Indians* 281–82; Hassrick, *The Sioux* (cited n. 42, p. 87, above) 198; *Memories of the American Folk-Lore Society* 32 (1938) 199.

with earth or sand, or rolls around in the sand, after taking a sweat bath. This too we have seen to be a common means of disguise among primitive hunters.

In this way we can also explain the origin of another curious feature of Greek sport. It was customary for Greek wrestlers, after they had anointed themselves with olive oil, to powder themselves with sand or dust. Lucian, in the work referred to above,[102] gives two (contradictory) reasons for the practice. On the one hand, he claims that the sand counteracts the effect of the olive oil (which is true) and allows the opponent a firm grasp, thereby giving the wrestler good practice at escaping from so firm a grasp. This is, of course, nonsense, as the same effect could be produced by dispensing with the olive oil in the first place. Also it does not explain—although, to be fair, Lucian is not concerned to explain—why wrestlers in the Congo, who do not use olive oil, rub their hands and arms with dust before they compete.[103] On the other hand, Lucian claims that the sand is beneficial because it "is thought to stop profuse sweating, to prolong strength, and to prevent harm to [the wrestlers'] bodies from the wind blowing on them when their pores are open." Lucian does not explain how sand affects the wrestler's strength, or why it is beneficial to inhibit sweating, or why the pores should be closed against the wind only during exercise. But we have dealt with a similar explanation earlier of the effects of olive oil. Both sand and olive oil close the pores and inhibit perspiration. While this is of no particular benefit to the wrestler, it can be crucial to the success of the hunter. It is clear that the Greek athlete was doing precisely the same thing as the aborigine kangaroo hunter who smears himself with clay and the Navaho tribesman who rolls in the sand after his sweat bath.

Disguise, camouflage and various forms of concealment are among the oldest and most widespread technological resources of our species. Their association with the hunt through countless millennia of human existence has assured their survival in various ritual connections. Disguise is memorialized in the mimetic action of the drama, which was formalized by the Greeks, but has much more primitive origins, and in a number of mythical accounts. The myth referred to above, of the dismemberment of Dionysus and his subsequent revivification by means of a cauldron has clear associations with the ritual of blood sacrifice.

102. Lucian, *Anacharsis* 29. The translation below is from S. G. Miller, *Arete* (Chicago, 1979) 23.
103. Diem, *Weltgeschichte des Sports* 85.

Before the Titans murdered Dionysus, we are told, they deceptively smeared their faces with gypsum.[104] It is not clear why they should have disguised themselves or how the gypsum aided the deception. This feature of the myth is sometimes explained in terms of the terror inspired by the spectral appearance of artificially whitened faces. But it is also possible to account for it as a survival of primitive hunting practice. For the medical writer Celsus tells us that gypsum was one of the preferred substances to use in order to prevent excessive perspiration,[105] and we have seen that such substances are important elements of the hunter's disguise. Interestingly, it happens that it is precisely gypsum that is reported as the earliest form of facial disguise in the Greek theater.[106] This substance, then, was originally used on account of its value in inhibiting perspiration. But, when hunting ceased to be the primary means of securing food, this value was less highly prized. Since, however, the use of gypsum had been associated with success, and since it was perhaps vaguely recollected that this success had something to do with disguise and concealment, the application of gypsum came to be localized on the face. The practice survived among the earliest comic actors and in the myth concerning Dionysus, the patron of the drama. It would be interesting to trace the connections between the origins of drama and primitive hunting practice, for it is in the latter that mimesis was born. But that is a subject to be pursued at another time and by someone else. Let us now quit this brief excursus and return to the immediate topic of our inquiry.

Another feature of Greek sport that is particularly striking to those encountering Greek athletics for the first time is the complete nakedness of the athlete when he competed or exercised. For it was the practice of the Greeks throughout most of antiquity that all male participants in track and field sports, as well as jockeys in horseraces (charioteers traditionally wore long white tunics), competed in the nude. In fact the words *gymnastics* and *gymnasium* both come from Greek words the basic element of which is the adjective *gymnos*, "lightly clad" or "naked." From references in literature and from the numerous representations of athletes in the visual arts, it is clear that the latter is the signification of the word in connection with sport. But it was not always the case that Greek athletes competed in the nude. The earliest literary references to

104. Nonnus, *Dionysiaca* 6.169–70.
105. Celsus, *On Medicine* 3.19.2.
106. A. Pickard-Cambridge, *Dithyramb, Tragedy and Comedy,* second edition (Oxford, 1962) 74, quoting "Plutarch," *On the Sayings of the Alexandrians* 30.

sport in ancient Greece occur in the *Iliad*, which is, indeed, the earliest surviving European work of literature. In the description of the boxing match that took place at the funeral games for Patroclus, Homer tells us that Tydeus, the companion of the boxer Euryalus, helped the latter on with his "belt" before the match began. And Homer goes on to say that, after all the preparations for the match had been made, the two contenders "strode into the middle of the ring, girt up." And the same expression is used a few lines later to describe the two competitors in the wrestling match.[107] The "belts" worn by these competitors were clearly loincloths, such as are occasionally depicted on later vase paintings being worn by older men engaging in athletics.[108] (It seems to have been regarded by the Greeks as disgraceful for an older man, but not a younger, to be seen naked.)[109] So, on the basis of the limited evidence available to us, it appears that it was conventional in the time of Homer (around 700 B.C.) for athletes to wear loincloths, whereas in, say, the fifth century B.C., it was customary for athletes to compete in the nude.

The Greeks themselves were aware of this change in their practice. The historian Thucydides, who himself lived at the end of the fifth century B.C., says that it was the Spartans who

> were the first to play games naked, to take off their clothes openly, and to rub themselves down with olive oil after their exercise. In ancient times even at the Olympic Games the athletes used to wear coverings for their loins, and indeed this practice was still in existence not very many years ago.[110]

And similarly in the following century Plato, when he suggests that the women of his ideal state should exercise in the nude, replies to potential critics by saying,

> we may remind them that it is not so long since the Greeks, like most foreign nations of the present day, thought it ridiculous and shameful for men to be seen naked. When gymnastic exercises were first introduced in Crete and later at Sparta, the humorists had their chance to make fun of them; but when

107. *Iliad* 23.683–85 and 710.
108. See, for example, the two black-figure vases from the end of the sixth century B.C. illustrated by Gardiner (*Athletics of the Ancient World*, pls. 163 and 182).
109. Cf. Tyrtaeus 10.26–27 West.
110. Thucydides, *The Peloponnesian War* 1.6.5., trans. Rex Warner (Harmondsworth, 1954).

experience had shown that nakedness is better uncovered than muffled up, the laughter died down.[111]

In order to account for the difference between the practice of athletes in Homer and that of the athletes in their own day, later Greeks gave various explanations. According to Dionysius of Halicarnassus, a writer of the first century B.C., Greek athletes did not compete in the nude until "the fifteenth Olympiad" (720 B.C.), at which time the Spartan runner Acanthus set the fashion for later times by appearing at the Olympic Games without the loincloth that had previously been customary.[112] Approximately two hundred years after Dionysius was writing, Pausanias attributed the origin of the practice of competing in the nude to the Megarian sprinter Orsippus, who won the one-stade foot race at the Olympic Games in 720 B.C. Pausanias suggests that Orsippus deliberately broke with prevailing practice because he realized that a naked man can run faster than one encumbered with a loincloth.[113] The tradition associating the origin of the practice with the fifteenth Olympiad seems to have been fairly strong; the version in Dionysius appears to derive from a desire to accommodate that tradition to the belief that the practice of competing in the nude was an invention of the Spartans. But there was another tradition as well. It is preserved in the work of Isidore of Seville, who lived in the seventh century after Christ. According to his account, at a race that took place in Athens one of the runners had the misfortune of having his loincloth slip down and trip him. In order to prevent this from happening in the future, the magistrate in charge of the games laid down a ruling that henceforth athletes were to be allowed to compete in the nude.[114]

The effect of these various and divergent accounts is to prove to us that the ancient Greeks, who were always very fond of assigning names to the "inventors" of otherwise unexplained customs, were themselves unaware of the reason for the practice. Modern scholars have not been much more successful in explaining why the Greeks adhered to the (seemingly dangerous) practices of boxing, wrestling and horseback riding without the benefit of any protective clothing. Věra Olivová, for example, tries to show that nakedness in athletics goes hand in hand with the rise of the individual in sixth- and fifth-century Greece, a phe-

111. Plato, *The Republic* 452c–d, trans. F. M. Cornford (Oxford, 1941).
112. Dionysius of Halicarnassus, *Roman Antiquities* 7.72.3.
113. Pausanias, *Description of Greece* 1.44.1.
114. Isidore of Seville, *Origins* 18.17.2.

nomenon that has been widely studied and analyzed. According to her sociological approach, "nudity . . . was for the Greeks a statement of individuality."[115] But we are entitled to wonder why this statement of individuality was made specifically in connection with athletics. It is also not entirely clear why individuality cannot be adequately proclaimed by a man wearing a loincloth. Further, as Dr. Olivová is well aware, the representations of athletes in sixth- and fifth-century art are not individualized portraits, but idealized representations of a type. Another sociological explanation of nudity has been essayed by James Arieti, according to whom Greek athletes dispensed with the loincloth in order to demonstrate to the world the "self-control and decorum" expected of participants in athletic contests. "Since the athletes were entirely stripped, stripped even of the loincloth the barbarians continued to wear, if they yielded to whatever sexual arousal they may have felt, it would have been blushingly apparent to all the spectators."[116] The evident inadequacy of this explanation—How much sexual arousal is a man subject to, after all, while throwing the discus?—makes it unnecessary to spend time refuting it. I refer to it merely to show the lengths to which scholars have gone to account for the phenomenon.

As we have seen, and as is so often the case, when a practice cannot otherwise be explained, recourse is had to religion or ritual or (preferably) both. In the case of nakedness among Greek athletes, this is an attractive avenue of approach. We sometimes lose sight of the fact that the athletic competitions in ancient Greece that were organized on a regular basis were in fact part of a religious festival. This is true not only of the Olympic Games and the other Panhellenic, or Crown, Games, but of all the formal athletic competitions for which we have evidence. So it is not inappropriate to look to the religious and the ritual sphere in order to explain some of the features of Greek sport. The historian Hermann Bengtson accordingly (correctly) regards the story about Orsippus and the other accounts of the origin of the practice as later rationalizations. For him the practice of competing at the Olympic Games and elsewhere in the nude is a case of "ritual nakedness."[117] The only reference that Bengtson gives is to an essay by the Nazi Richard Harder, who does not in fact discuss "ritual nakedness" at all, but merely points

115. Olivová, *Sports and Games* 131–33.
116. J. A. Arieti, "Nudity in Greek Athletics," *Classical World* 68 (1975) 431–36. For the self-control to which Arieti refers, see K. J. Dover, *Greek Homosexuality* (Cambridge, Mass., 1978) 96–97.
117. H. Bengtson, *Die Olympischen Spiele in der Antike* (Zurich, 1971) 59.

out that nakedness, as something that is removed from the everyday, is the mark of a special occurrence.[118] Some evidence does exist, however, that entitles us to speak of ritual nakedness. Pierre Vidal-Naquet points out that there were some initiation rites in ancient Crete in which the young man is said to have been naked before he assumed the warrior's arms symbolic of his entry into manhood.[119] Walter Burkert uses the same expression that Bengtson had used when he says, in connection with an Athenian festival in honor of Artemis, "seclusion and even cultic nakedness . . . are typical initiation motifs."[120] And a curious piece of advice is given to farmers by the early didactic poet Hesiod: "Sow naked, plough naked, reap naked."[121] We cannot be certain either in the case of the initiation rituals or in Hesiod's prescription whether the Greek word *gymnos* means "naked" or "lightly clad."[122] But there are parallels from other societies for nakedness in connection with initiation (as I can attest from my early fraternity days) and, as far as agricultural practice is concerned, there are representations in Greek art of men sowing and ploughing in the nude, and Frazer gives some examples of nakedness as part of vegetation rituals in other cultures.[123]

But unless we invoke "vegetation magic," we have not explained anything by referring the practice of the ancient Greek athlete to ritual nakedness. And even if we were to resort to that discredited concept, we would still have to explain vegetation magic in order to have any confidence that we were not accounting for one mysterious procedure by reference to another. Some scholars, noting, as we have done, that nakedness is a common feature of initiation rituals, have seen in initiation ritual the origin of many features of Greek religion and Greek sport.[124] This is in some ways a very attractive hypothesis, for many elements of initiation ritual can be seen in connection with sport, both in ancient Greece and elsewhere: nakedness or simply change of clothes,

---

118. R. Harder, *Eigenart der Griechen: Eine kulturphysiognomische Skizze* (Freiburg im Breisgau, 1949) 13–17.

119. P. Vidal-Naquet, *Le Chasseur noir: Formes de pensée et formes de société dans le monde grec* (Paris, 1981) 168.

120. Burkert, *Greek Religion* 263. The German original reads "*kultische Nacktheit.*"

121. Hesiod, *Works and Days* 391–92.

122. In the case of the festival in honor of Artemis to which Burkert refers, however, there is archaeological evidence for (female) nakedness; see L. Kahil, "L'Artémis de Brauron: Rites et mystère," *Antike Kunst* 20 (1977) 86–98 with pls. 18–21.

123. M. L. West, *Hesiod: Works and Days* (Oxford, 1978) 257–58; Frazer, *Magic Art* I 248, 282–83. See also J. Heckenbach, *De nuditate sacra sacrisque vinculis,* Religionsgeschichtliche Versuche und Vorarbeiten 9.3 (Giessen, 1911).

124. See especially Jeanmaire, *Couroi et Courètes,* and Brelich, *Paides e parthenoi.* For nakedness, see Jeanmaire 531, 559, 566 and Brelich 31 with n. 60, 200.

ritual bath or baptism, the application of substances to the body, period of taboo, flagellation, scarification and various other bodily (often sexual) mutilations.[125] And we may add that the age classifications that were a feature of many Greek athletic festivals are reminiscent of the similar classifications that characterize intiation rituals.[126] But it is difficult to see what we have gained by deriving features of sport from initiation ritual. For, despite the fact that initiations have been widely studied, and despite the fact that they display clearly defined characteristics, it cannot be said that they have been any more adequately "explained" than vegetation magic. To account for sport in terms of initiation ritual is no more satisfactory than to account for it in terms of any other form of cultic practice. Even if we could confidently assert that initiation ritual is historically prior to sport, we would still be left with the question of why features of initiation ritual persisted in connection with sport. Still, the features that sport and initiation ritual share are so striking that there is surely some historical connection between the two. It will by now be obvious that these features are precisely those that we have accounted for as survivals of primitive hunting practice, and it is reasonable to suppose that both sport and initiation ritual, like many other elements of religious ritual, derive from the practices of the primitive hunters. It is not the case that sport originates in initiation ritual. (Nor is it the case that initiations derive from sport.) Rather both are, like blood sacrifice, collateral descendants of hunting ritual.

Let us then see whether it is possible to explain the nakedness of Greek athletes in the same way that we have explained sweat baths, wreaths, cauldrons and the use of olive oil and dust, namely as a survival of primitive hunting practice. At first sight it would appear that stripping naked is as foolish and dangerous on the hunt as in the wrestling pit. And indeed hunters are not so foolish as to leave themselves entirely unprotected. But just as the Cherokee strips off his ordinary clothing and wears only a loincloth or a pair of shorts when playing lacrosse, so it is very common among other American Indians to wear nothing but a loincloth while engaged in sport or while hunting. (We must leave out of account here the hunters of Australia and of equatorial Africa,

125. Nakedness, change of clothes: Jeanmaire 442, 518, 578 and Brelich 31 with n. 60. Bath: Brelich 66 n. 48, 369–70, 376–77. Substances: Brelich 31, M. L. West, *The Orphic Poems* (Oxford, 1983) 155 n. 49. Taboo: Brelich 31 with n. 58. Mutilations: Jeanmaire 213, 417, 511 and Brelich 34 with nn. 89–93; see also discussion below of infibulation and the use of the strigil.

126. Jeanmaire 211, 502–7 and Brelich 39–41 with nn. 136–45, 454.

whose everyday dress is negligible, and those of the far north, who must wear heavy clothing while hunting as a protection against the cold.) What is the reason for this practice? The answer was given by Ishi, the famous Yahi Indian who was the last representative of his tribe:

> In hunting deer, Ishi was particularly careful in the observance of several essential precautions. He would eat no fish on the day prior to the hunt, because the odor could be detected by deer, he said; nor would he have the odor of tobacco smoke about him. The morning of the hunt Ishi bathed himself from head to foot, and washed his mouth. Eating no food, he dressed himself in a shirt, or breech clout. Any covering on the legs made a noise while in the brush, and a sensitive man rather favored cautious walking. While Ishi was proud of his shoes acquired in civilization, he said they made a noise like a horse.[127]

Once again, we see that the fasting and the purification are by no means ritual matters. Rather they are rational and pragmatic measures designed to enhance the likelihood of success. Another precaution that Ishi observed was to make sure that he did not approach his prey from the windward. According to his civilized physician and friend Saxton Pope, "his observance of this rule was almost an obsession." But this is no more obsessive behavior than Dr. Pope's washing his hands before performing surgery.

Equally pragmatic is Ishi's (and other primitive hunters') clothing. But Ishi gives only part of the reason for hunting so lightly clad. Not only does ordinary clothing rustle and make a noise that might alert the prey to the hunter's presence, it may also catch on shrubs and branches, making still more noise and possibly impeding the hunter's progress. But most important of all, it is impossible completely to remove the wearer's smell from his clothes. There is no point in the hunter's bathing his body and refraining from eating fish in order to prevent the deer from smelling him, if he is only going to put his everyday clothing on before he hunts. We must remember that the primitive hunter is not, like us, accustomed to changing his clothes twice a day. Nor is he accustomed to washing his clothes in chemical detergents advertised as having the capacity to make one's wardrobe smell like springtime. As Meuli recognized, this is the reason for the practice of putting on clean

---

127. S. T. Pope in R. F. Heizer and T. Kroeber, eds., *Ishi the Last Yahi: A Documentary History* (Berkeley, 1979) 195. Similar points about the noise of clothing and footwear are made in a didactic poem, attributed to Oppian, written at the beginning of the third century after Christ (*Cynegetica* 1.101–8).

vestments for sacrifices and for other ceremonial rituals.[128] But, since the evidence that Meuli was using came primarily from the hunters within the Arctic Circle, he was prevented from realizing that this is the origin of ritual nakedness as well. Ideally, the hunter should wear nothing at all. But in practice he wears as little as he can consistent with his own safety. In northern climates, since he must be fully clothed, he makes sure to wear new clothes on the hunt, clothes not yet permeated with his own scent. In warmer regions the hunter can dispense with all clothing, or can restrict himself to a loincloth. Since stripping had been associated for millennia with success in securing food, it became ritualized as the importance of hunting receded. Near-nakedness became a symbol of effectiveness and potency, for which reason many American Indians stripped before they engaged in ritual sacrifice of energy on the lacrosse field.[129] Also, once its original purpose had been forgotten, it aquired a "magical" ability to ensure a plentiful supply of food. In an agricultural society, the result is a farmer who takes his clothes off before sowing, ploughing and reaping in order that the yield be improved. As far as Greek sport is concerned, we know that in Homer's time the athlete wore in competition what Ishi wore on the hunt. The "belt" of Homer's boxers and wrestlers served the same pragmatic function as the loincloth of the primitive hunter. But boxing and wrestling are ritual acts, and we are familiar with the intensification that characterizes ritual. At some time between the age of Homer and the end of the sixth century B.C., the traditional costume of the Greek athlete became even more extreme in its scantiness.

I do not suffer from the delusion of believing that I have "explained" the nakedness of Greek athletes. I have merely followed in the footsteps of Karl Meuli and have shown that the practice has its origin in the habits of the primitive hunters. Geoffrey Kirk has intelligently pointed out a limitation of Meuli's (and, by extension, my own) method, namely, that pointing to the origins or antecedents of a practice is not the same as understanding the practice.[130] Our earlier discussion of the nature of ritual, based upon the science of ethology, was designed to meet this objection at least in some measure. Ritual behavior simply

128. Meuli, "Griechische Opferbräuche" 226–27, 253–54, 264 (= *Gesammelte Schriften* II 950–51, 981, 993).
129. See Culin, *Games of the North American Indians* 570 (Missisauga), 571 (Passamaquoddy), 575 and 581 (Cherokee), 593 (Seneca), 598 (Choctaw), 607 (Muskogee), 614 (Dakota).
130. G. S. Kirk in *Entretiens sur l'antiquité classique* 27 (1980) 70–72.

persists and is transformed because it finds other needs to fill. But Kirk's criticism is justified. It is still necessary to explain why the Greek athlete dispensed with his loincloth, whereas the Cherokee ballplayer, for example, and the Japanese sumo wrestler do not. And it is necessary to explain why the Greek athlete took this radical step when he did, and not, say, in the ninth or the fourth century B.C. But this is not the place for an investigation of this interesting matter, and I hope the reader will forgive me for not pursuing it here. For it is a sociological and historical problem of interest only to students of Greek sport and Greek culture. Our concern here was not with the epiphenomenal—for such I consider to be the change from the wearing of a loincloth to total nakedness—but with those features of Greek sport that give evidence of its ritual nature. The features I have examined so far have for the most part been those that we can trace back to their origins among the practices of primitive hunters. These provide what I consider to be convincing proof that sport among the ancient Greeks was indeed a ritual act. Inasmuch as some of these features—crowning with fillets and crowns of vegetation, prizes of cauldrons—have explicit connections with sacrifice, and inasmuch as sacrificial ritual is itself a survival of primitive hunting practice, we have a strong likelihood (although not, I will grant, conclusive proof) that the ritual of Greek sport was indeed a form of sacrifice, namely the sacrifice of human energy. To these features we can add a few more, which we can treat much more cursorily and which will strengthen this likelihood still further.

One of the events in which the Greeks competed, in the Olympic Games and at other athletic competitions, was a race in armor. In this event the contestants raced over a fixed distance, but they were not naked as in other footraces. Rather they were required to wear the heavy armor of a warrior, normally consisting of a shield, a helmet and a pair of greaves. The most prestigious and demanding of these races in armor took place at the Boeotian town of Plataea, about thirty miles from Athens. This was the site of the decisive battle of the Persian War in 479 B.C., and the prestige of this race was attributed in antiquity in part to the fact that it took place at a festival established to commemorate this greatest of Greek military victories.[131] It was considered to be a particularly demanding race on account of the distance run (we are not told the exact length of the race) and on account of the equipment that

---

131. Philostratus, *On Gymnastics* 8; Pausanias, *Description of Greece* 9.2.6; Strabo, *Geography* 9.2.31. For the festival, see Plutarch, *Life of Aristeides* 21.

the competitors were required to carry. Unlike the smaller round shield used in other races in armor (the standard piece of protective equipment for the Greek soldier of the classical period), the shield prescribed for this race was a large oval one that reached from the wearer's neck to his ankles. Now, this kind of shield was a relic of a previous age. It is referred to in the Homeric poems, but had ceased being used by soldiers long before the time of the battle of Plataea.[132] Either, therefore, the officials in charge of this festival deliberately and consciously revived what they knew to be an archaic practice, or this race, with its obsolete shield, is in fact older than 479 B.C. and was taken over by the newly established festival in honor of the battle of Plataea. The former possibility is inherently improbable—Why revive a feature of warfare characteristic of the heroic age that was incompatible with the style of warfare at the time of the battle being celebrated?—and it is likely that the race at Plataea owed its prestige not only to the association with the battle but also to its great antiquity.[133]

There was another feature of the race in armor at Plataea that also, I believe, attests to its antiquity. Victors in this race were discouraged from competing again. According to Philostratus, it was the law that anyone who had been crowned victor at Plataea and who subsequently competed and failed to win, was subject to a penalty of death. H. A. Harris simply does not believe that this was the case, and he brands Philostratus' account a "legend." According to Harris, "this sounds like a story told by old hands in athletic dressing-rooms to gullible youngsters." But gullible youngsters had nothing to fear from a provision that applied only to former victors in a race that took place every four years, and Jüthner is undoubtedly right to regard the law as genuine.[134] The significance of the law is that it reinforced the status of the athletic victor as sacrificial victim. There have, of course, been societies in which sports and human sacrifice were explicitly connected. One thinks of Etruscan and Roman gladiatorial combats and certain Mexican and South American ritual ball games. And there have been attempts to explain sport as arising out of original human sacrifice, which evolved into armed combat and was further sublimated in the form of various com-

132. A. M. Snodgrass, *Arms and Armour of the Greeks* (London, 1967) 55. But Snodgrass is mistaken in saying that this kind of shield did not exist in the classical period. It existed, but only (so far as we can tell) for use in the race at Plataea.

133. For the preservation of Bronze Age practices at another festival at Plataea, see Burkert, *Structure* 132–34.

134. Harris, *Greek Athletes* 75; Jüthner, *Philostratos über Gymnastik* 201.

petitive sports.[135] But, as Meuli points out, it is difficult to see what exactly the mechanism was that accounts for the development from human sacrifice to organized combat.[136] I think it is more reasonable to assume that the development was in the other direction. In other words, gladiatorial combats and other contests designed to end in the death of one or more of the participants represent an intensification of the ritual sacrifice of energy. Indeed, it may be the case that in general human sacrifice is an intensification of ritual mutilations like circumcision and subincision, rather than that these mutilations are "substitutes" for, or symbolic forms of, human sacrifice. At any rate, there seems to be a vague recollection of ritual combat preserved in Homer's description of the funeral games for Patroclus.[137] And it would seem that the rule concerning victors in the race in armor at Plataea was also a reflection of a time when the ritual sacrifice of energy was occasionally intensified to the point of actually involving human sacrifice.

There are other (and perhaps only superficial) connections between sport and sacrifice. We have earlier referred to the necessity that the sacrificial animal be, or be considered as, a willing victim, and to the appropriateness of athletes in a footrace vying with one another to be the first to the altar. One aspect of the willingness of the sacrificial victim was that, despite the fact that it was normally a domesticated animal, it was by a conventional fiction considered to be wild.[138] The ox to be sacrificed, for example, would be one that had not been yoked to the plough and had not performed the tasks characteristic of its domestication. Likewise, slaves were forbidden from competition at the Olympic Games and, indeed, at most athletic festivals in the Greek world. But it is not only at the explicitly religious festivals that slaves were forbidden from participating in sports. By chance the fourth-century orator Aeschines preserves for us an Athenian law stating that "a slave may not exercise or oil his body in the palaestras."[139] The palaestra was the ancient Greek equivalent of our YMCA. An Athenian man would go to the palaestra to wrestle with his friend much as we today would go to a gym or a country club to swim or to play golf or tennis. In other words, the palaestra was the scene, not of serious athletic competition

135. E.g., L. Malten, "Leichenspiel und Totenkult," *Mitteilungen des Deutschen Archäologischen Instituts: Römische Abteilung* 38–39 (1923–24) 300–340.
136. *Die Antike* 17 (1941) 193 (= *Gesammelte Schriften* II 886).
137. *Iliad* 23.798–825.
138. Burkert, *Homo Necans* 16.
139. Aeschines, *Against Timarchus* 138; cf. Plutarch, *Life of Solon* 1.6.

at the highest level, but of informal, recreational sport. But even sport at this level is a form of sacrifice, and to allow slaves to engage in it would be equivalent to using inferior and unsatisfactory victims in sacrifices to the gods.

Animal sacrifice in Greece normally took place to a musical accompaniment. The instrument that provided the music for sacrifice is commonly referred to in English as a flute, but was in fact a reed instrument more like an oboe than a flute. This instrument, with its characteristic double body, is frequently depicted on vase paintings showing scenes of sacrifice. On a red-figure mixing bowl, for example, from the end of the fifth century B.C., we see a young ram being led to the altar for sacrifice (Fig. 17). To the left is a musician playing a double pipe. A similar musician is shown on a red-figure vase from the first half of the fifth century, now in the British Museum (Fig. 19). He accompanies the roasting of the sacrificial meat on the altar. An even older, black-figure painting depicts a procession to the altar, with the double-pipe player immediately behind the sacrificial bull (Fig. 21). Indeed, the double pipe was such a common feature of ancient Greek sacrifice that the fifth-century historian Herodotus, when he describes the peculiarities of the sacrificial practice of the Persians, singles out the fact that they do not use the pipe as an accompaniment to their sacrifices.[140] The same instrument that was used by the Greeks as an accompaniment to sacrifice (as well, of course, as for other purposes) was also used in athletic contexts.[141] A black-figure vase in the Metropolitan Museum in New York shows a pair of boxers practicing their moves to the rhythmic accompaniment of music provided by a wreathed double-pipe player (Fig. 18). But it was not only while practicing that Greek athletes used the music of the double pipe. Pausanias and Philostratus tell us that such musical accompaniment also existed during competitions.[142] So that when, as is often the case, a double-pipe player is shown in vase paintings in association with athletic activity, it is not always possible to tell whether the scene represented is one of actual competition or of informal practice in the palaestra. Such scenes appear, for example, on two vase paintings, one in Copenhagen and one in Basel. The former shows a musician playing for a javelin thrower, a discus thrower and a

140. Herodotus, *Histories* 1.132.1.

141. W. J. Raschke, "Aulos and Athlete: The Function of the Flute Player in Greek Athletics," *Arete* 2 (1985) 177–200.

142. Pausanias, *Description of Greece* 5.7.10, 6.14.10; Philostratus, *On Gymnastics* 55; cf. Jüthner, *Philostratos über Gymnastik* 301.

long jumper (Fig. 20). The latter depicts a long jumper jumping to the accompaniment of a double pipe while two other long jumpers look on (Fig. 22).

I have chosen these two vase paintings in part because they also illustrate a rather curious feature of Greek athletics that has received little attention and that it will be worth while to mention here. The three pentathletes on the vase from Copenhagen and the long jumper to the left of the double-pipe player on the vase from Basel all have penises that look as though they are curling back on themselves. These young men have practiced what is commonly (but inappropriately) referred to as infibulation. That is, they have tied a string—not shown in the paintings—around the prepuce and then fastened the string about their waist so that the penis is held in the position illustrated. The string is shown, however, in an Etruscan fresco that is, like most Etruscan frescoes depicting athletic scenes, heavily influenced by Greek vase paintings (Fig. 23). This practice is frequently shown in representations of athletics on Greek vases, and there are a few references to it in the literary sources. These references are conveniently collected by Julius Jüthner and Eric Dingwall, but neither gives a satisfactory explanation for the origin of the practice.[143] The most recent treatment of the subject is in Waldo Sweet's article on protection of the genitals in Greek sport, but Sweet's discussion of the Greek athlete's reason for practicing infibulation is inconclusive. In spite of the fact that his article is concerned with protection of the genitals, Sweet does not make clear whether he believes that Greek athletes practiced infibulation for the purposes of protection or for some other reason.

Male infibulation is much less widely known and practiced than female infibulation, which has attracted considerable attention in recent years, particularly among feminist writers, who regard it as yet another instance of the exploitation of women.[144] In female infibulation the labia are pierced and a pin or clasp (Latin *fibula*) is inserted in order to pre-

---

143. Jüthner, s.v. "Infibulatio," *Paulys Real-Encyclopädie der classischen Altertumswissenschaft* IX (Stuttgart, 1916) 2543–48; E. J. Dingwall, *Male Infibulation* (London, 1925). The latter also includes references to a great deal of comparative ethnographic material, but he ignores the North American examples discussed below.

144. F. P. Hosken, *Female Sexual Mutilations: The Facts and Proposals for Action* (Lexington, Mass., 1980); R. Saurel, *L'Enterée vive: Essai sur les mutilations sexuelles féminines* (Geneva, 1981); L. P. Sanderson, *Against the Mutilation of Women: The Struggle to End Unnecessary Suffering* (London, 1981); R. H. D. Abdalla, *Sisters in Affliction: Circumcision and Infibulation of Women in Africa* (London, 1982); A. El Dareer, *Woman, Why Do You Weep?: Circumcision and its Consequences* (London, 1982).

vent sexual intercourse. Men can be infibulated in the same way and, clearly, for the same purpose. The prepuce is pierced and a pin or ring is inserted. There is evidence for this practice (to which the term *infibulation* is appropriately applied) among the Romans, but not among the Greeks. But surely the Greek practice of (temporarily) tying up the foreskin with a string presupposes the practice of binding the foreskin on a more permanent basis. The purpose of infibulation is to enforce (involuntary) chastity by making intercourse physically impossible. We have seen that (voluntary) abstention from intercourse is common in many societies for a period of time prior to hunting, warfare and athletic competition. Particularly in a society in which nudity in public was commonplace, infibulation could thus become a conspicuous symbol of an individual's commitment to chastity. This is the significance of a vase painting, which I have chosen not to illustrate, showing a young man whom the god Poseidon is pursuing with amorous intent. The young man's flight from the god and the fact that he is infibulated in the same manner as the athletes whom we have examined show that he has no intention of allowing himself to be seduced.[145] Even in the case of the more permanent type of infibulation—that is to say, in which a metal ring is employed—a symbolic function can be added to the pragmatic. For, if we are to believe the undocumented assertion of P. C. Remondino, "among the Greek monks" the ring "not only is a sure badge of chastity, but its weight and size is very often increased so as to render it an instrument of penitence, and considerable rivalry exists at times in this regard."[146] In other words, for the athletes and, to a certain extent, for the monks, the practice became ritualized. From being a means of ensuring chastity and, hence, success in hunting, warfare and athletics, infibulation among athletes became a symbol of chasteness and, through its symbolic value rather than from any actual capacity for preventing intercourse, it became a means of enhancing the athlete's performance. Greek athletes tied strings around their foreskins for no other reason than that they felt that by doing so they could throw the javelin farther or run faster.

145. For an excellent illustration of this vase, see S. Kaempf-Dimitriadou, *Die Liebe der Götter in der attischen Kunst des 5. Jahrhunderts v. Chr.,* suppl. 11 of *Antike Kunst* (Bern, 1979) pl. 5. Other clear and readily accessible examples of this form of infibulation are: a runner in the race in armor (Olivová, *Sports and Games* 103), a giant carrying an enormous stone (*Strena Helbigiana* [Leipzig, 1900] 116), and Heracles wrestling the Nemean lion (*Corpus Vasorum Antiquorum,* Deutschland 20 [= München 5] [Munich, 1961] pl. 240.5).

146. P. C. Remondino, *History of Circumcision from the Earliest Times to the Present* (Philadelphia, 1891) 54.

Confirmation of the above comes, surprisingly, from a practice of the Navaho Indians. In their account of the Navaho sweathouse, Kluckholm, Hill and Kluckholm[147] record that "before entering, men pulled their prepuce over the glans of the penis and tied it; according to the myth explaining the origin of the sweathouse blindness resulted from a failure to observe this custom." There are two interesting features in this account: the relationship between infibulation and the sweathouse, and the connection between blindness and the transgression of the custom. The fact that blindness is specified as the penalty indicates that the offense is thought of as a sexual one. For blindness is a very common punishment in mythic accounts for sexual impropriety.[148] But what sexual impropriety is involved in entering the sweathouse with the glans of the penis exposed? As we have seen, the reason for entering the sweathouse is the expectation of removing the impurities from the body. These impurities take the form of a liquid that is either identical with the sweat or is carried out of the body along with the sweat. But there is a need to ensure that it is only the pernicious fluids that are removed from the body, and the tying up of the prepuce is the convenient means of preventing the evaporation of the vital fluids during the sweat bath. Ancient Greek athletes and Navaho Indians, then, engaged in this practice for the same purpose, namely to prevent the escape of vital fluids and thereby to conserve the strength of the individual. Roman actors and singers practiced infibulation in order to preserve their voices, and the first-century writer Celsus states that infibulation was practiced sometimes for the sake of the voice and sometimes for the sake of general physical well-being.[149] Now, among the Romans, infibulation consisted of the insertion of a large pin or metal ring, so that sexual intercourse was prevented. (Of course a more radical means of preventing the loss of vital fluids is castration, and the operatic castrati of more recent times were clearly the descendants—figuratively speaking—of the ancient Italian *infibulati*.) But the temporary binding of the prepuce, attested for the Greeks and the Navaho, does not exist primarily for the purpose of preventing intercourse. This is proved by two considerations. In the first place, since the man infibulated *himself* and did so, moreover, only with a piece of string, he could just as easily, should the urge present itself, remove the impediment himself. In the second place, what need would there be of taking specific measures to

147. *Navaho Material Culture* (cited n. 100, p. 105, above) 321.
148. See, for example, G. Devereaux, *Journal of Hellenic Studies* 93 (1973) 40–49.
149. Celsus, *On Medicine* 7.25.3; Jüthner, "Infibulatio" 2544.

prevent sexual intercourse during athletic competition or in a sweat-house frequented only by men? It may, perhaps, be suggested that it was precisely in order to inhibit homosexual encounters that these customs were instituted. But the practice of the Mandan Indians indicates that this kind of infibulation had, rather, a symbolic value, and was intended, as suggested above, to preserve, and perhaps even to augment, the individual's strength.

In 1832 George Catlin witnessed the O-kee-pa, an annual ceremonial of the Mandans of the Upper Missouri River, and he described it in great detail. Here is a portion of his account of the preparations that the participants in the bull-dance underwent:

> The first ordeal they all went through . . . was that of *Tah-ke-way ka-ra-ka* (the hiding man), the name given to an aged man, who was supplied with small thongs of deer's sinew, for the purpose of obscuring the *glans* secret, which was uniformly done by this operator . . . by drawing the prepuce over in front of the glans, and tying it secure with the sinew, and then covering the private parts with clay, which he took from a wooden bowl, and, with his hand, plastered unsparingly over.[150]

Figure 24 shows a young man after having been thus infibulated. The plastering with clay, the impersonation of the buffalo and several other features of this ritual are now familiar to us as survivals of primitive hunting practice. Similarly the sweat bath, the context in which the Navaho infibulated themselves, has been shown to be another such survival. The existence of infibulation in these contexts, as well as in connection with Greek athletics, makes it all but certain that it too had its origin among the practices of prehistoric hunters, who must have used infibulation of this kind in association with the nearly universal period of ritual abstinence before the hunt.

This leads us—although the transition will not be immediately obvious—to the final feature of Greek sport that we need to consider. As we have seen above, it was customary for the Greek athlete to anoint his body with olive oil before he competed or practiced. Then, when he was finished, he would scrape the olive oil, along with the accumulated sweat, dirt and blood, off his body with a bronze implement known as a strigil. As far as I am aware, no one has questioned his reasons for

---

150. G. Catlin, *O-kee-pa: A Religious Ceremony and Other Customs of the Mandans* (New Haven, Conn., 1967) 58. The account was originally published in 1867.

doing this. One can only assume that, once scholars have accepted the practice of anointing in the first place, they must feel that it is perfectly reasonable that the athlete should remove the olive oil after it has served its purpose. Of course, it is perfectly reasonable, but it is not therefore self-evident why the athlete, if he wished to remove olive oil from his body, should *scrape* it off, nor is it obvious why he should use an instrument of just this shape (Fig. 25). In any case, as soon as the athlete had scraped himself off with the strigil, he took a bath, using a sponge and any of the various chemical soaps that were widely known among the Greeks.[151] Sponges and strigils are commonly represented side by side in Greek vase paintings,[152] so that it is clear that scraping and washing were not alternative means of removing the oil from the body. Rather, the athlete used both strigil and sponge. One would think that the bath would be sufficient to rid the body of the olive oil, sweat, dirt and blood, and therefore that the use of the strigil was motivated by considerations other than those commonly assumed.

One possibility is that the strigil was used to scrape the olive oil off because there was a desire to preserve the matter that had been removed, a procedure that would have been impossible if it had been washed off. In fact, the Roman author Pliny tells us that the offscourings from the gymnasia were used as salves for inflammation and other diseases of the skin.[153] The "magical" properties of these scrapings are perhaps also hinted at in a legend preserved in the work of the geographer Strabo, according to whom the matter scraped off by the Argonauts after they had exercised at Elba became congealed and turned into the pebbles on the shore of that island.[154] Not only olive oil but, as we have earlier seen, sweat also is sometimes felt to have "magical" properties, and this may have contributed to the value placed upon athletes' offscourings. But it is likely that the preservation of this matter was a secondary development, and that the original purpose of scraping it off with a strigil is to be sought elsewhere. A clue is provided by the author of one of the treatises that comprise the Hippocratic Corpus. In recommending procedures for bathing acutely ill patients, he prescribes that "sponges are preferable to strigils." In other words, the gentler action of the sponge should be substituted, in the case of the sick, for the astringencies of the strigil. But the acutely ill had presumably not

151. Ginouvès, *Balaneutikè* 141–43.
152. Ginouvès, *Balaneutikè* 96–97.
153. Pliny, *Natural History* 28.50–52.
154. Strabo, *Geography* 5.2.6; cf. Apollonius of Rhodes, *Argonautica* 4.655.

been anointing themselves for exercise in the first place, and there should have been no need for them to use a strigil to scrape off nonexistent oil. It appears, then, that the strigil was used simply for scraping the skin, regardless of whether the skin had been anointed. This is confirmed by a passage in a work, earlier attributed to Aristotle, called *Problems*. In it the question is posed, "Why is it that perspiration flows more freely in the case of those who have scraped themselves off with a strigil than in the case of those who allow it (i.e., the perspiration) to remain (i.e., on their skin)?" Clearly what is envisioned here, and perhaps in the passage from the Hippocratic Corpus as well, is the scraping off, not of olive oil, but of perspiration.[155]

Apparently the use of the strigil was simply a prelude to the bath, regardless of whether one had been exercising previously, and regardless of whether one's body was coated with olive oil. It may even be that it is a mistake to consider the use of the strigil in connection with athletic practice, as I am doing here. It may be the case, for example, that the strigil came to be thought of primarily as an instrument for removing olive oil from the body because of an accidental juxtaposition: the use of the strigil was a prelude to the bath, and athletes, who happened to be in the habit of anointing themselves, were frequenters of the bath. Let us, then, for the moment not think of the use of the strigil as the last item in a sequence, but as the first. Instead of considering the sequence anointing-exercising-scraping, let us consider the sequence scraping-bathing-anointing. For this was the normal procedure in the Greek bath: one scraped one's body with a strigil (or with a sponge, in the case of the acutely ill), washed the body with soap, water and a sponge, and then coated the body lightly with olive oil.[156] We have earlier seen that bathing and smearing the body with vegetable matter, animal fats and the like are features of primitive hunting practice, and it is therefore not surprising to recall that we have encountered a similar sequence before. In preparation for their lacrosse game, the Cherokees bathe frequently in a river and then undergo the painful ritual ordeal of scratching.

> The shaman then gives to each player a small piece of root, to which he has imparted magic properties by the recital of certain secret formulas. Various roots are used, according to the whim

---

155. "Hippocrates," *Regimen in Acute Diseases* 65; cf. Pliny, *Natural History* 31.131. "Aristotle," *Problems* 2.12.

156. Ginouvès, *Balaneutikè* 144.

of the shaman, their virtue depending entirely upon the ceremony of consecration. The men chew these roots and spit out
the juice over their limbs and bodies, rubbing it well into the
scratches; then going down to the water, plunge in and wash
off the blood, after which they come out and dress themselves
for the game.[157]

Here we have the sequence scratching-anointing-bathing, rather than
the sequence scraping-bathing-anointing, which is what we find among
the Greeks. Another difference between the practice of the Cherokees
and that of the Greeks is that, in the case of the former, this procedure
is a preliminary to athletic activity, whereas in the case of the latter it
followed such activity.

But these differences do not obscure the fact that these two procedures are identical both in their essence and in their origin. We have
seen that the prehistoric hunter bathed and anointed himself before the
hunt in order to conceal his scent from his quarry. When the original
purpose of these practices was lost sight of, they became ritualized, and
they survived because it was felt that they were conducive to success,
not only in the hunt, but also in connection with war and sports. Presumably it was felt that these practices were conducive to success because they imparted strength, speed, endurance and so forth. They
could be engaged in beforehand, to augment the hunter's, warrior's or
athlete's faculties, or afterwards, to restore him following exertion. The
Cherokee bathes and anoints himself before, and bathes himself after,
the game. The Greek anointed himself before, and bathed and anointed
himself after, engaging in athletic activity. Now, what has all this to do
with the use of the strigil among the Greeks? To begin with, it should
be clear from its association with athletics, bathing and anointing that
the function of the strigil was analogous to (but not identical with) that
of the turkey-bone instrument used in the Cherokee scratching ordeal.
We have not yet established the rationale for the latter with certainty.
In a matter like this, certainty is indeed too much to hope for, but we
can suggest a reasonable hypothesis. After the original purpose of
anointing had been forgotten, it must have been believed that the substance with which men were in the habit of anointing themselves itself
had the "magical" power of increasing their strength. Since the substance was applied to the surface of the skin, and since its effect was

157. Mooney, "Cherokee Ball-Play" 122 (= Culin, *Games of the North American
Indians* 581).

apparently produced on the muscles, sinews and other internal parts of
the body, it was felt to be more efficacious to score the surface of the
skin and to allow the substance more direct access to its target. Frazer
cites a number of parallels to this sort of practice from other societies
and from other contexts. Among the Yoruba tribes of Africa, mothers
would drive evil demons out of the bodies of their sick children by
making incisions that were filled, much to the discomfort of the already
suffering children, with green peppers and spices. Members of the Basuto and Barotse tribes are purified after contact with the dead by having magical substances rubbed into incisions made in their hands and
foreheads, respectively. Swiftness of foot is imparted to East African
elephant hunters by rubbing gunpowder into incisions made in their
toes. Among the Tupi Indians of Brazil, after the executioner had performed his office "he made incisions in his breast, arms, and legs, and
other parts of his body with a saw made of the teeth of an animal. An
ointment and a black powder were then rubbed into the wounds, which
left ineffaceable scars so artistically arranged that they presented the
appearance of a tightly-fitting garment."[158] This appears to be the origin of the practice of tattooing, which exists today for "aesthetic" purposes rather than for the purpose of repelling evil spirits. But the effect
is the same: it is practiced in hopes of enhancing one's personal success.
The latest refinement in this procedure is the development of a surgical
technique, advertised by local physicians (who thus proclaim their affinity with the shamans and "medicine-men" of other societies), whereby
women's eye makeup can be permanently implanted in the skin.

It will be objected, however, that the shape of the strigil and the use
to which it is put provide no evidence of its origin as an instrument of
scarification. But we are now in a position to shed some light on the
origin and nature of the strigil. These instruments were a favorite possession of men in ancient Greece, and they are so commonly found as
offerings in graves in the classical period that archaeologists were surprised at not finding any when they excavated a burial pit on the island
of Rheneia earlier in this century. What they found instead were about
fifty iron sickles, and John Boardman has perceptively recognized that
these sickles are in fact the missing strigils.[159] Elsewhere also, as Board-

---

158. Frazer, *Taboo* 106 (Yoruba), 107 (Basuto, Barotse, elephant hunters), 180
(Tupi).
159. J. Boardman, "Sickles and Strigils," *Journal of Hellenic Studies* 91 (1971) 136–
37. Boardman's perception is supported by considerations brought forth by J. K. Anderson, "Sickle and *Xyele*," *Journal of Hellenic Studies* 94 (1974) 166.

man points out, strigils are indistinguishable from sickles. In the sanctuary of Artemis Orthia at Sparta, for example, sickles were dedicated as the prizes in contests for which strigils would appear to be more appropriate. Now, what is the significance of this revelation? It is possible, I suppose, that the people of Rheneia and Sparta, who have no particular historical connection with one another, for some reason (independently?) modified the form of the strigil, which is itself of mysterious origin, so as to resemble a common agricultural implement. But it seems far more likely, particularly considering the notorious conservatism of the Spartans, that the sickle shape was the original form, and that the strigil developed its characteristic shape (but not at Sparta or Rheneia) at a relatively late date. Objects that can be certainly identified as strigils are not found before the last half of the sixth century B.C. But Boardman notes that a number of sickles from Perachora that are as old as the seventh or eighth century B.C. are so designed that they would be inappropriate for agricultural use, but could presumably be used for the purpose normally served by a strigil. If sickles, or implements nearly indistinguishable from sickles, had been used by the Greeks for scraping the body before the strigil developed its characteristic shape, that would account for the fact that archaeologists have not been able to find strigils dating to the time before the late sixth century B.C.

But we still seem to be far from any connection between sickles and strigils on the one hand and instruments of scarification on the other. That is because the sickle of archaic and classical Greece (and the strigil that developed from it) has a smooth edge. But the Greeks were aware of an earlier, and perhaps the earliest, form of the sickle, namely that with a denticulated or serrated cutting edge. This type of sickle, with which we may compare the Cherokee turkey-bone comb and the Tupi "saw made of the teeth of an animal," is known to have been used in Greece in the Bronze Age. A specimen was discovered in the recent excavations at Mycenae,[160] and another, from Cyprus, has long been in the collection of the Metropolitan Museum of Art in New York.[161]In the archaic and classical periods, however, use of the denticulated sickle seems to have ceased, although it survived in the memory of the Greeks, as we know from representations in works of art and from references in literature. In Hesiod's version of the succession-myth of the gods, we read that Cronus castrated his father Uranus with an adamantine sickle

160. *Bulletin de Correspondance Hellénique* 91 (1967) 658, fig. 15.
161. G. M. A. Richter, *Greek, Etruscan and Roman Bronzes* (New York, 1915) 439.

"with jagged teeth."[162] On two engraved Boeotian fibulae from the end of the eighth century B.C. we see Heracles' companion Iolaus attacking the Lernaean Hydra with a serrated sickle.[163] According to the usual version of the story, the instrument with which Perseus beheads Medusa is a sickle, and this sickle is sometimes represented in vase paintings as denticulated.[164]

These three myths—the castration of Uranus, the subduing of the Hydra and the decapitation of Medusa—have a particular affinity beyond the presence in all three of the unusual weapon.[165] In the first, the blood that spurts from the severed genitals of Uranus is the seed that engenders the Erinyes and the Giants, and the organs themselves, floating upon the sea, produce a foam out of which the goddess Aphrodite is born. The mythical Hydra was supposed to have many heads, and for each one that was cut off, two more grew in its place. When Perseus cut off the head of Medusa, Chrysaor and the horse Pegasus were born. In other words, in each instance the cutting off of part of the adversary's body resulted either in the regeneration of that part or in the generation of some new creature.[166] It is this that makes the sickle the appropriate weapon in these three myths. For the normal, agricultural purpose of the sickle is to cut the grain at harvest time, some of which is replanted to generate the harvest for the following year.

Just as sowing is requisite for reaping, so reaping is requisite for sowing. This is the paradox that lies at the root of sacrifice.[167] Something must be squandered so that more can be produced. Grain must be spilled upon the ground to enable more grain to grow. The father must lose his seed and, ultimately, his life for the son to live. And the son, in turn, attempts to preserve his own vital force by sacrificing it. Cronus emasculates his father with the jagged sickle, only to become a father himself. In the next generation the sickle has become a strigil,

162. Hesiod, *Theogony* 175, 180; cf. 161–62.
163. See R. Hampe and E. Simon, *The Birth of Greek Art* (Oxford, 1981) 66, with pls. 92 and 93; Burkert, *Structure* 80–82.
164. See, for example, K. Schefold, *Götter- und Heldensagen der Griechen in der spätarchaischen Kunst* (Munich, 1978) 83, pl. 96, and 85, pl. 99.
165. Strigils, too, are sometimes lethal weapons: Philostratus, *On Gymnastics* 18; Xenophon, *Anabasis* 4.8.25. For the latter, see Anderson, "Sickle and *Xyele*."
166. We may compare the myth, attested only in a late source (Apollodorus, *The Library* 1.6.3), according to which Zeus fights Typhon with a sickle. The latter wrests the sickle from Zeus and severs the sinews of his hands and feet, hiding them in a bearskin. Later, Hermes and Aegipan steal the sinews and restore them to Zeus, who ultimately subdues Typhon.
167. See Guépin, *Tragic Paradox,* passim; Burkert, *Homo Necans,* esp. 290–91; Onians, *Origins of European Thought* 113–15.

and Cronus' son reenacts his father's violence. Zeus has become an athlete, and he overthrows his father in a wrestling match at the future site of the Olympic Games.[168] But the past is never forgotten. The topographical feature that dominates Olympia is the Hill of Cronus. Before the games begin, the athletes, standing before the awesome statue of Zeus Upholder of Oaths, had to swear an oath by the severed genitals of a wild boar.[169] And the prize won at the games, worn by the victorious Zeus himself in the cult statue by Phidias, was a crown of wild olive cut from the sacred olive tree by a young man, both of whose parents were still living, wielding a golden sickle.

The Olympic Games, and the myths associated with the Olympic Games, embody the various elements of sport that we have seen to be derived from primitive hunting ritual, many of which are also connected with Greek sacrificial ritual. It will be worth while to review those elements briefly here by way of conclusion. To begin with, the athlete who was victorious at the games was given woolen fillets and a crown of wild olive to wear. We have suggested that these, like the fillets and crowns of vegetation worn by priests in ancient Greece, were survivals of the practice of the primitive hunter who disguised himself from his prey by wearing animal skins or leafy camouflage. For a period of thirty days prior to the opening of the games, the athlete was required to subject himself to the close supervision of the Olympic officials, who regulated his diet and his course of training during this period. This has been connected with the taboo period commonly associated with ritual sacrifice, which originated among primitive hunters who were concerned to preserve their strength by conserving their bodily fluids and whose diet was guided by a desire to avoid consuming foods before the hunt that were likely by their odor to alert the prey to the presence of the hunter. Before he competed in the games, the athlete would strip off his clothes, bathe, anoint his body with olive oil and, in many instances, sprinkle sand or dirt over himself, all practices originally designed to secure success on the hunt by reducing the risk of the hunter's scent being perceived by the animal prey. That these practices were now no longer associated with the hunt, but rather accompanied such activities as jumping, running and throwing the discus, shows that they were now ritual acts.

168. Pausanias, *Description of Greece* 5.7.10, 8.2.2; cf. Aeschylus, *Agamemnon* 171.

169. Pausanias, *Description of Greece* 5.24.9. For the meaning of the word *tomia* ("genitals"), see P. Stengel, *Opferbräuche der Griechen* (Leipzig, 1910) 78–85.

It may be argued that, even granting that the activities accompanying sport are themselves rituals, it is not thereby demonstrated that sport is itself a ritual act. But, in the first place, we saw in Part One that it is easiest to account for the persistence of sport by recognizing its ritual character. In the second place, the numerous associations between sport and sacrificial ritual in ancient Greece encourage us in the belief that sport is itself a form of sacrificial ritual. In addition to the elements that sport and sacrificial ritual share as common descendants of hunting practice (fillets, wreaths of vegetation, bathing, change of clothing, dietary and sexual taboos), we have seen that there is a more explicit connection between sport and sacrificial ritual in the frequent use of sacrificial vessels as prizes in athletic competitions. While cauldrons are not attested as prizes at the Olympic Games in the historical period, there is evidence that such prizes were given at Olympia in earlier times, and the myth of Pelops, who was revivified after his dismembered body was boiled in a cauldron, associates Pelops with the founding of the Olympic Games. And, in general, the associations of sport in ancient Greece are with ritual sacrifices. The athletic events of the Olympic Games were held in conjunction with a sacrifice at the tomb of Pelops and another at the altar of Zeus. Elsewhere in Greece, sporting events were connected with religious festivals, the central act of which was a ritual sacrifice, and the purpose of which was the maintenance of the continuity of life. The exhilaration that accompanies sport is precisely parallel to that which accompanies sacrifice: by a traumatic and enervating act, the sacrificer has given birth to renewed life and restored vigor.

Selected Bibliography

Brelich, A. *Paides e parthenoi*. Rome, 1969.

Burkert, W. *Structure and History in Greek Mythology and Ritual*. Berkeley, 1979.

————. *Homo Necans: The Anthropology of Ancient Greek Sacrificial Ritual and Myth*. 1972. English translation. Berkeley, 1983.

————. *Greek Religion*. 1977. English translation. Oxford, 1985.

Culin, S. *Games of the North American Indians*. Annual Report of the Bureau of American Ethnology 24. Washington, D.C., 1907.

Damm, H. "Vom Wesen sogenannter Leibesübungen bei Naturvölkern: Ein Beitrag zur Genese des Sportes." *Studium Generale* 13 (1960) 1–10.

Diem, C. *Weltgeschichte des Sports und der Leibeserziehung*. Stuttgart, 1960.

Eibl-Eibesfeldt, I. *Love and Hate: The Natural History of Behavior Patterns*. 1970. English translation. New York, 1974.

————. *Ethology: The Biology of Behavior*. 1967. English translation, second edition. New York, 1975.

Frazer, J. G. *The Magic Art and the Evolution of Kings*. 2 vols., third edition. London, 1935.

————. *Taboo and the Perils of the Soul*. Third edition. London, 1935.

Gardiner, E. N. *Athletics of the Ancient World*. Oxford, 1930.

Gaster, T. H. *Myth, Legend, and Custom in the Old Testament*. New York, 1969.

Ginouvès, R. *Balaneutiké: Recherches sur le bain dans l'antiquité grecque*. Paris, 1962.

Grupe, O., D. Kurtz, and J. M. Teipel, eds. *The Scientific View of Sport: Perspectives, Aspects, Issues*. Berlin, 1972.

Guépin, J.-P. *The Tragic Paradox: Myth and Ritual in Greek Tragedy*. Amsterdam, 1968.

Guttmann, A. *From Ritual to Record: The Nature of Modern Sports*. New York, 1978.

Harris, H. A. *Greek Athletes and Athletics*. London, 1964.

————. *Sport in Greece and Rome*. London, 1972.

Hubert, H., and M. Mauss. *Sacrifice: Its Nature and Function.* 1899. English translation. Chicago, 1964.

Hye-Kerkdal, K. "Wettkampfspiel und Dualorganisation bei den Timbira Brasiliens." In *Die Wiener Schule der Völkerkunde: Festschrift,* ed. J. Haekel, A. Hohenwart-Gerlachstein, and A. Slawik, 504–33. Vienna, 1956.

Jeanmaire, H. *Couroi et Courètes.* Travaux et Mémoires de l'Université de Lille 21. Lille, 1939.

Jensen, A. E. *Myth and Cult Among Primitive Peoples.* 1951. English translation. Chicago, 1963.

Jüthner, J. *Philostratos über Gymnastik.* Leipzig, 1909.

Körbs, W. "Kultische Wurzel und frühe Entwicklung des Sports." *Studium Generale* 13 (1960) 11–21.

Leeuw, G. van der. *Religion in Essence and Manifestation.* 1933. English translation. London, 1938.

Lorenz, K. *On Aggression.* 1963. English translation. New York, 1966.

Mandell, R. D. *Sport: A Cultural History.* New York, 1984.

Meuli, K. "Der Ursprung der olympischen Spiele." *Die Antike* 17 (1941) 189–208. (= *Gesammelte Schriften* II 881–906)

———. "Griechische Opferbräuche." In *Phyllobolia für Peter von der Mühll,* 185–287. Basel, 1946. (= *Gesammelte Schriften* II 907–1018)

———. *Gesammelte Schriften.* 2 vols. Basel, 1975.

Mooney, J. "The Cherokee Ball-Play." *American Anthropologist* 3 (1890) 105–32.

Nimuendajú, C. *The Eastern Timbira.* University of California Publications in American Archaeology and Ethnography 41. Berkeley, 1946.

Olivová, V. *Sports and Games in the Ancient World.* 1984. English translation. London, 1984.

Onians, R. B. *The Origins of European Thought about the Body, the Mind, the Soul, the World, Time, and Fate.* Second edition. Cambridge, 1954.

Opler, M. E. "The Jicarilla Apache Ceremonial Relay Race." *American Anthropologist* 46 (1944) 75–97.

Sweet, W. E. "Protection of the Genitals in Greek Athletics." *Ancient World* 11 (1985) 43–52.

Ueberhorst, H., ed. *Geschichte der Leibesübungen.* Vols. I–II. Berlin, 1972–78.

Weiler, I. *Der Sport bei den Völkern der alten Welt.* Darmstadt, 1981.

Index

Compositor: G & S Typesetters
Text: 10/13 Galliard
Display: Galliard
Printer: Braun-Brumfield, Inc.
Binder: Braun-Brumfield, Inc.